ISBN 1-891112-74-0

Table of Contents

Modeling with Styles

INTRODUCTION

Styles allow you to save multiple formatting characteristics under a name so that you can format your worksheet quickly and consistently. You simply define the styles you would like to use in your models and apply them when you would like to format cells. Once you have set up your styles, you can make them available in other workbooks. Excel has a limited number of pre-defined styles, but they have not been designed with the avid financial modeler in mind!

This section explains how to:

- Define a style
- Apply a style
- Edit and delete existing styles
- Use styles in other Excel files
- Make styles available in other Excel files
- Define styles for financial modeling purposes

DEFINING A STYLE

This section will show you the generic steps necessary to define a style. The *Styles for financial modeling purposes* section on page 9 will show you examples of styles you may want to define in your model.

To define a style, ensure you have an Excel file open and:

1. Select F̲ormat, S̲tyle from the menu. The Style dialog box will appear:

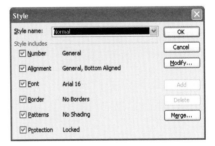

2. In the S̲tyle name box enter a name for the style.

3. Check the formatting category or categories you would like to attach to the style.

4. Select the M̲odify button to specify the formats associated with the style. The Format Cells dialog box will appear:

5. Choose the desired formats using the Format Cells dialog box and choose OK.

6. Choose OK on the Style dialog box.

APPLYING A STYLE

There are a number of ways to apply styles:

- Using the Style dialog box
- Using the Style drop down box
- Copying and pasting
- Copying and pasting special formats

APPLYING A STYLE USING THE STYLE DIALOG BOX

Using the Style dialog box is probably the most logical but also the most cumbersome way to apply a style. To apply a style using the Style dialog box:

1. Select the cells you would like to apply the style to.

2. Choose Format Style from the menu to show the Style dialog box.

3. Select the desired style from the Style name drop down box.

4. Choose OK.

APPLYING A STYLE USING THE STYLE DROP DOWN BOX

One of the quickest ways to apply a style is via the Style drop down box. The Style drop down box is not available by default, so you must first add it to your toolbar.

Adding the Style drop down box to an existing toolbar

To add the Style drop down box to an existing toolbar:

1. Select Tools, Customize from the menu. The Customize dialog box will appear:

2. Select the Commands tab.

3. Select the Format category.

4. Locate the Style drop down box from the list of commands as shown below.

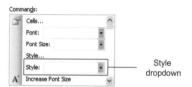

Style dropdown

5. Drag the Style drop down box to the desired location on your toolbar.

A logical place to put this command is to the left of the Font type drop down box on the Formatting toolbar as shown below:

Style dropdown

Applying a style using the Style drop down box
To apply a style using the Style drop down box:

1. Select the cells you wish to format.

2. Select the desired style using the Style drop down box. Your cells will be formatted in accordance with the style!

Rather than using the mouse to select the Style drop down box, you can also use the ALT + ' keyboard shortcut to activate the Style drop down box. Once the Style drop down box is activated, simply use your up and down cursor keys to select the style you wish to apply. Once selected, press the ENTER key to apply the style. Instead of using the arrow keys to select the desired style you can also start typing the style name into the Style drop down box. Once the style you wish to apply appears, press the ENTER key to apply the style.

APPLYING A STYLE USING COPY AND PASTE

Copying and pasting to apply a style provides a quick and dirty solution to applying styles as you are building your model. To apply a style using copy and paste:

1. Select a cell containing the style you wish to copy.

2. Press CTRL and C to copy the cell.

3. Select the cell or cells you wish to copy the style to.

4. Press ENTER or CTRL + V to paste.

Note: Using this method will copy all attributes of the source cell (formatting, contents and any comments). After you paste, you can delete the contents of the cell using DELETE or replace the old content with a new value. I would not recommend using this method if your source cell includes comments.

APPLYING A STYLE USING COPY AND PASTE SPECIAL

This method is very similar to the method described above, but it only pastes the formatting attributes (including the style) of the cell. To apply a style using this method:

1. Select a cell containing the style you wish to copy.

2. Press CTRL and C to copy the cell.

3. Select the cell or cells you wish to copy the style to.

4. Choose Edit, Paste Special from the menu. The Paste Special dialog box will appear.

5. Choose the Formats option button.

6. Choose OK.

Note: Instead of following steps 4-6 above, you can hold down ALT and press E, S, T in sequence, followed by ENTER.

EDITING AN EXISTING STYLE

Rather than defining a new style, you may wish to change an existing style. To edit an existing style:

1. Select Format, Style from the menu.

2. Select the style you wish to edit from the Style name drop down box.

3. Check the formatting category or categories you would like to attach to the style.

4. Select the Modify button to specify the formats associated with the style. The Format Cells dialog box will appear.

5. Choose the desired formats using the Format Cells dialog box and choose OK.

6. Choose OK to save the changes to the style.

DELETING AN EXISTING STYLE

To delete an existing style:

1. Select Format, Style from the menu.

2. Select the style you wish to delete from the Style name drop down box and choose Delete.

Note: You cannot delete the Normal style. If you delete the Comma, Currency, or Percent styles, you won't be able to use the Comma Style, Currency Style, or Percent Style buttons on the Formatting toolbar.

MAKING STYLES AVAILABLE IN DIFFERENT EXCEL FILES

Styles will only be available in the file you set them up in. Once you have defined your styles there are a number of ways you can make them available in other files. You can:

- Import styles from another file
- Save styles in a general template
- Save styles in the default workbook template

IMPORTING STYLES FROM ANOTHER FILE

The easiest but least convenient way to make your styles available in another file is to import them from the Excel file that contains them. This process is called merging styles. To merge styles:

1. Open the file containing the styles you wish to import.

2. Open and go to the file you want to receive the styles.

3. Choose Format, Style from the menu. The Style dialog box will appear.

4. Choose the Merge button. The Merge dialog box will appear showing a list of other open Excel files.

5. Select the file containing the styles you wish to import.

6. Choose OK.

7. If you see the following dialog box, choose Yes to merge styles that have the same name.

8. Choose OK to close the Style dialog box.

You can now start using the styles in the file that received them.

SAVING STYLES IN A GENERAL TEMPLATE FILE

An alternative way to make styles available in another file is to save them in a template file. When you open a new file based on the template you will have access to the styles. To save styles in a template file:

1. Open a new file and define the styles as described in the *Defining a style* section on page 1 or merge styles from an existing file as described above.

2. Once you have defined your styles, choose File, Save As from the menu.

3. Type a filename for the template in the File name edit box.

4. Choose Template from the Save as type drop down box.

After choosing Template from the Save as type drop down box, you will automatically be directed to the template folder, which is where all templates should be stored for easy access. The path of this folder is usually:

C:\Documents and Settings\<*user_name*>\Application Data\Microsoft\Templates

5. Choose the Save button to save the template and its styles.

6. Close the file.

Now that you have saved the styles in a template file, you can access them with ease by opening a new file based on the template. To open a new file based on the template:

1. Choose File, New from the menu. The New Workbook task pane will appear as shown below.

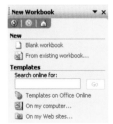

Note: You must choose <u>F</u>ile, <u>N</u>ew and not the New button on the toolbar to see the New Workbook pane.

2. Choose the "On my computer" link. The Templates dialog box will appear.

3. Ensure the General tab is selected and select the template containing the desired styles. A new workbook will open containing your styles.

SAVING STYLES IN THE DEFAULT WORKBOOK TEMPLATE

When you choose the New button on the toolbar or use CTRL + N, Excel opens a new file based on the default workbook template. If you save your styles in the default workbook template, you will always have access to them when you open a new file as described above. To save styles in the default workbook template:

1. Open a new file and define the styles as described in the *Defining a style* section on page 1 or merge styles from another file as described in the *Importing styles from another file section* on page 6.

2. Once you have defined your styles, choose <u>F</u>ile, Save <u>A</u>s from the menu.

3. In the File <u>n</u>ame edit box enter "Book" as the filename – you must use this name.

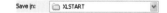

4. Choose Template from the Save as <u>t</u>ype drop down box.

5. Using the Save <u>i</u>n drop down box select the xlstart folder.

Note: The xlstart folder path is usually:

C:\Program Files\Microsoft Office\Office11\XLStart

6. Choose <u>S</u>ave to save the template and its styles.

7. Close the file.

Now that you have saved your styles in the default workbook template, you can access them by simply opening a new file using the New button or CTRL + N.

Note: Your styles will only be available in models built based on the default workbook template. To make styles available in existing models built based on a different template, use the merge style command described in the *Importing styles from another file* section on page 6.

STYLES FOR FINANCIAL MODELING PURPOSES

There are a number of styles you should create which will become an essential part of your financial modeling toolkit. Once you have set these styles up, you can use them in other models (refer to the *Making styles available in different Excel files* section on page 6 for a reminder on how to do this). This section will address how to set up these styles.

NORMAL STYLE

The Normal style is the default style which is attached to all cells in a new file. When you edit the Normal style, the associated formatting will therefore apply to all cells in a new file.

A user-friendly financial model will have most of its numbers formatted in the following way:

- One decimal place
- Thousand separators
- Negative numbers in parentheses
- Zero numbers shown as 0.0

The three numbers: 14568.456; -6778.23; and zero will therefore be shown as:

	A	B
1	14,568.5	
2	(6,778.2)	
3	0.0	

You should therefore edit the Normal style so that it uses the following custom number format string (for more information on custom number formats, refer to the

Custom number formats section on page 22 of this chapter):

$$\#,\#\#0.0\_)\ ;\ (\#,\#\#0.0)$$

This means that a number entered into your model will have the formatting characteristics shown above. To set up this style:

1. Choose F<u>o</u>rmat, <u>S</u>tyle from the menu.

2. Ensure the Normal style is selected.

3. Choose the <u>M</u>odify button. The Format Cells dialog box will appear.

4. In the Format Cells dialog box, select the Number tab and choose the Custom category as shown below.

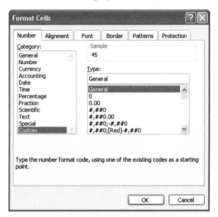

5. Enter the custom number format string:

$$\#,\#\#0.0\_)\ ;\ (\#,\#\#0.0)$$

in the <u>T</u>ype field.

6. Choose OK to close the Format Cells dialog box and return to the Styles dialog box.

7. Confirm that the custom number format code appears next to the <u>N</u>umber category as shown below:

8. Choose OK to close the Style dialog box.

Every cell in your workbook should now have this format attached to it. It is now the default cell format for this workbook as you amended the default style.

PERCENT STYLE

Your models will also use percentages for assumptions and ratios. Once again, Excel has a percent style but it should be amended to make it more suitable for modeling purposes. The percent style should have the following formatting characteristics:

- One decimal place
- A percent symbol (%) after the number
- Negative numbers in parentheses
- Zero percent shown as 0.0%

The three numbers 0.125, 0 and -1 will therefore be shown as:

	A	B
1	12.5%	
2	0.0%	
3	(100.0%)	

Amend the existing percent style so that it uses the following custom number format string (for more information on custom number formats, refer to the

Custom number formats section on page 22 of this chapter):

```
0.0%_);(0.0%)
```

The percent symbol (%) in the custom number format string formats the number as a percent. However, as with all number formatting, the underlying number does not change. In the example above, the underlying numbers are still 0.125, 0 and -1.

To set up this style:

1. Choose Format, Style from the menu.

2. Select the Percent style from the Style name drop down box.

3. Ensure only the Number category is selected, as shown below:

4. Choose the Modify button. The Format Cells dialog box will appear.

5. In the Format Cells dialog box, select the Number tab and choose the Custom category as shown below.

6. Enter the custom number format string:

```
0.0%_);(0.0%)
```

in the Type field.

Type:

0.0%_);(0.0%)|

7. Choose OK to close the Format Cells dialog box and return to the Styles dialog box.

8. Confirm that the custom number format code appears next to the Number category as shown below:

☑ Number   0.0%_);(0.0%)

9. Choose OK to close the Style dialog box.

Here are a few points about the percent style we should address here before moving on:

- The Percent style is not a default style. You will therefore need to apply it to cells you would like to format as a percent (refer to the *Applying a style* section on page 2 for a reminder on how to do this).
- If you type a number as a percent into a Normal style cell (this assumes you have amended the Normal style as suggested above), it will appear as a decimal. For example if you type 10% into a Normal style cell, it will appear as 0.1. You will therefore need to apply the Percent style to the cell.
- If you have the "Enable automatic percent entry" option active, you can type a number into a Percent style cell and it will divide the underlying number by 100 but will appear as a percent. For example, if you type 1 it will appear as 1%. If the option is not active, it will appear as 100%. To activate this option: choose Tools, Options from the menu; select the Edit tab; check the Enable automatic percent entry option.

BLUE STYLE

The Blue style is a simple but useful style that changes the font color of a cell to blue. It is common practice to color code input, historical numbers blue to show that they are input, historical numbers.

To define the Blue style:

1. Choose Format, Style from the menu. The Style dialog box will appear.

2. Enter the style name "Blue" into the Style name box

Style name: Blue   ∨

3. Ensure only the Font formatting option is selected in the Style Includes check boxes.

4. Choose Modify. The Format Cells dialog box will appear.

5. Select the Font tab.

6. Choose the blue color on the second row of the color palette using the Color drop down box as shown below:

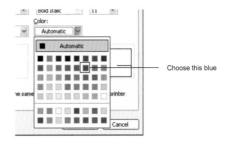

Choose this blue

7. Choose OK to close the Format Cells dialog box and return to the Style dialog box.

8. Choose OK to close the Style dialog box.

INPUT STYLE

The Input style is designed for the assumptions in your model. The Input style has the following formatting characteristics:

- Light yellow background
- Cell border
- Blue font color

To define the Input style:

1. Choose Format, Style from the menu. The Style dialog box will appear.

2. Enter the style name "Input" into the Style name box.

3. Ensure only the Font, Border and Patterns formatting options are selected from the Style Includes check boxes as shown below.

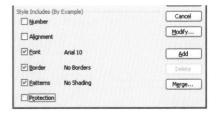

4. Choose Modify. The Format cells dialog box will appear.

5. Select the Font tab and choose the blue font color using the Color drop down box.

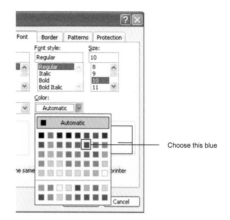

Choose this blue

6. Select the Border tab and choose the Outline button.

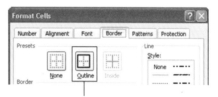

Choose the outline button

7. Select the Patterns tab and choose the light yellow color from the Cell shading color palette as shown below:

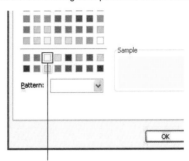

Choose this light yellow color

8. Choose OK to close the Format Cells dialog box and return to the Style dialog box.

9. Choose OK to close the Style dialog box.

The Date style is another essential for your modeling toolkit. This section addresses how to set up a date style with the following formatting characteristics:

- Day as a number with leading zeros (01-31)
- Abbreviated month (Jan-Dec)
- Abbreviated year (00-99)

Entering 31 December 07 into a cell would therefore return:

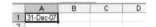

To set up the Date style:

1. Choose Format, Style from the menu.

2. Enter the style name "Date" into the Style name box.

3. Ensure only the Number formatting option is selected from the Style Includes check box as shown below.

4. Choose Modify. The Format Cells dialog box will appear.

5. Ensure the Number tab is selected and choose the Custom category.

6. Enter the following custom number format string in the Type box:

```
dd-mmm-yy
```

7. Choose OK to close the Format Cells dialog box and return to the Style dialog box.

8. Choose OK to close the Style dialog box.

MULTIPLE STYLE

The Multiple style adds the symbol "x" to the end of a number. You can use this style for valuation multiples, leverage multiples, coverage ratios, etc. To set up the Multiple style:

1. Choose Format, Style from the menu.

2. Enter the style name "Multiple" into the Style name box.

3. Ensure only the Number formatting option is selected from the Style Includes check box as shown below.

4. Choose Modify. The Format Cells dialog box will appear.

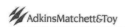

5. Ensure the Number tab is selected and choose the Custom category.

6. Enter the following custom number format string in the Type box:

```
#,##0.0 x_);(#,##0.0 x)
```

7. Choose OK to return to the Style dialog box.

8. Choose OK to close the Style dialog box.

MULTIPLE STYLE WITHOUT THE X

The Multiple style without the "x" can be used as part of a formatting effect where the multiples in the first row of your model have multiple signs, and the multiples in the other rows do not. An illustration of this is shown below:

	A	B	C
1	Company name	EV / EBITDA	PE
2	Orange inc	11.3 x	22.3 x
3	Blue inc	12.5	24.0
4	Green inc	11.1	21.9

The following custom number format string has been attached to a style to achieve this result:

```
#,##0.0_ _x_);(#,##0.0 _x)
```

To set up this style:

1. Choose Format, Style from the menu.

2. Enter the style name "Multiple_" into the Style name box.

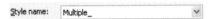

3. Ensure only the Number formatting option is selected from the Style Includes check box as shown below.

4. Choose Modify. The Format Cells dialog box will appear.

5. Ensure the Number tab is selected and choose the Custom category.

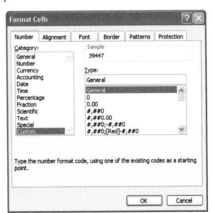

6. Enter the following custom number format string in the <u>T</u>ype box:

```
#,##0.0_  _x_);(#,##0.0 _x)
```

<u>T</u>ype:

#,##0.0_ _x_);(#,##0.0 _x)

7. Choose OK to return to the Style dialog box.

8. Choose OK to close the Style dialog box

SPECIAL UNDERLINE STYLE

The Special Underline style ensures that the width of an underline is consistent regardless of the number of digits a number has. As you can see from the illustration below, underlining the Profit before tax, Tax and Net income rows using CTRL + U produces underline widths to match the width of the number.

A	B	C	D	E	F
1	*Divisional income statement extract*				
2					
3		Division 1	Division 2	Division 3	Total
4	Profit before tax	12,000.0	34.0	453.0	12,487.0
5					
6	Tax	4,080.0	10.9	158.6	4,249.4
7	Net income	7,920.0	23.1	294.5	8,237.6
8					

Used with CTRL + U, the Special Underline Style produces an underline that spans the width of the cell as shown below:

A	B	C	D	E	F
1	*Divisional income statement extract*				
2					
3		Division 1	Division 2	Division 3	Total
4	Profit before tax	12,000.0	34.0	453.0	12,487.0
5					
6	Tax	4,080.0	10.9	158.6	4,249.4
7	Net income	7,920.0	23.1	294.5	8,237.6
8					

All cells containing the underlining have been formatting with this special underline style. The Special Underline style has the following custom number format string attached to it:

```
_  * #,##0.0_);_  * (#,##0.0)
```

Note: There is a double space between the underscore (_) and the astrix (*) on both sides of the semi colon (;).

To set up this style:

1. Choose F<u>o</u>rmat, <u>S</u>tyle from the menu.

2. Enter the style name "Underline" into the <u>S</u>tyle name box.

<u>S</u>tyle name: | Underline

3. Ensure only the <u>N</u>umber formatting option is selected from the Style Includes check box as shown below.

4. Choose <u>M</u>odify. The Format Cells dialog box will appear.

5. Ensure the Number tab is selected and choose the Custom category.

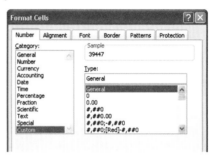

6. Enter the following custom number format string in the <u>T</u>ype box:

```
    _  * #,##0.0_);_  * (#,##0.0)
```

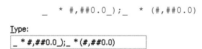

7. Choose OK to return to the Style dialog box.

8. Choose OK to close the Style dialog box.

To see the style work, apply the style to cells containing values, and then underline the cells using the Underline button on the toolbar or CTRL + U.

CUSTOM NUMBER FORMATS

WHAT IS A CUSTOM NUMBER FORMAT?

Custom number formats allow you to design your own number formats. To have easy access to your custom formats it is advisable to attach them to styles.

NUMBER FORMAT STRING

You construct a number format by specifying a series of codes as a number format string. You enter the string in the Type field under the Custom category of the Number tab in the Format Cells dialog box as shown below.

A custom number format string has four sections, each separated by a semi-colon:

```
Positive; Negative; Zero; Text
```

You can specify different number format codes for positive, negative and zero values. If you use the first three sections of the string, the first will apply to positive numbers, the second to negative numbers and the third to zeros. If you use all four sections, the last applies to text stored in the cell.

The following custom number format string specifies a different number format for each section:

```
[Green]General; [Red]General; [Black]General; [Red]General
```

It takes advantage of the fact that colors have special codes. A cell formatted with this custom number format will show positive numbers in green, negative numbers in red, and zero values in black. Any text entered into the cell will be displayed in red.

NUMBER FORMAT CODES

A custom number format string consists of a variety of number format codes. There are many number format codes available in Excel. The table below summarizes the main ones:

Code	Description
General	Displays the number in general format
#	Digit placeholder that displays only significant digits and does not display insignificant zeros
0 (zero)	Digit placeholder that displays insignificant zeros. If a number has fewer digits than there are zeros, the zeros are displayed. For example, the custom number format code 0000 would return 0307 if 307 was entered into the cell formatted with the code.
.	Decimal point
%	Percentage
,	Thousand separator
$ - + / () : space	Displays this character
_ (underscore)	Displays a space equal to the width of the next character
"text"	Displays the text inside the quotation marks
@	Text placeholder
[color]	Displays the characters in the color specified. The following text strings (not case sensitive) are acceptable: [Black], [Blue], [Cyan], [Green], [Magenta], [Red], [White], or [Yellow].

DATE NUMBER FORMAT CODES

Date custom number format codes allow you to create your own date formats. They are classified as number formats because each date is associated with an underlying number.

Code	Description
m	Displays the month as a number without leading zeros (1-12)
mm	Displays the month as a number with leading zeros (01-12)
mmm	Displays the month as an abbreviation (Jan-Dec)
mmmm	Displays the month in full (January-December)
mmmmm	Displays the first letter of the month (J-D)
d	Displays the day as a number without leading zeros (1-31)
dd	Displays the day as a number with leading zeros (01-31)
ddd	Displays the day as an abbreviation (Mon-Sun)
dddd	Displays the day in full (Monday-Sunday)
yy	Displays the year as a two digit number (00-99)
yyyy	Displays the year as a four digit number (1900-9999)

Circularities Under Control

INTRODUCTION

Circularities are a common phenomenon and can be the bane of a financial analyst's existence if they are not understood and controlled. The aim of this chapter is to explore and demystify circularities. It will provide essential tools and procedures you should use when working with or trying to avoid circular references.

WHAT IS A CIRCULAR REFERENCE?

A circular reference occurs when a formula directly or indirectly references its own cell. For example, suppose cell A2 contains the formula =A1+A2, then A2 would contain a direct circular reference. This is because the formula references the cell the formula is in.

Circular references can be intentional, but more often than not they are unintentional. When building a complex model with lots of references, it is very easy to create a circular reference by mistake, which will destabilize your model and lead to inaccurate results. However, under some very specific situations, you may want to create a circular reference. For example, the calculation of interest using average debt or cash balances will create an intentional circular reference. Good modelers know how to prevent unintentional circular references. They also know how to work with intentional circular references.

PREVENTING UNINTENTIONAL CIRCULAR REFERENCES

Circular references can be direct or indirect. Direct circular references are generally easy to identify and correct. An indirect circular reference is where one formula refers to another formula that refers to another formula that refers back to the original formula. Indirect circular references are probably the most common unintentional circular references; they're also the most difficult to solve. This is why it is important to adopt the procedures that this section will discuss to help prevent the creation of direct or indirect unintentional circular references.

While you are building your model, it is essential that you work with Excel's iteration setting deactivated. To deactivate this setting:

1. Choose Tools, Options from the menu. The Options dialog box will appear.

2. Select the Calculations tab.

3. Uncheck the Iteration check box.

4. Choose OK to close the dialog box.

Deactivating the iteration setting will ensure that Excel indicates the creation of a circular reference in the following ways:

- Displaying the circular message
- Displaying the circular indicator on the status bar
- Returning an unexpected zero as the result of a formula

These indicators are important warnings that you have created a circular reference. The warnings enable you to change the formula to avoid the circular reference.

If you model with the iteration setting activated, Excel will not display any warning message when you create a circular reference. Instead, it will simply attempt to iterate until it finds a solution. If you carry on modeling in this way, you may end up building a model riddled with unintentional circular references which will destroy the integrity of the model's output.

DISPLAYING THE CIRCULAR MESSAGE

If your iteration setting is deactivated and you write a formula that creates a circular reference, Excel will display the following warning message:

This message simply warns you that the formula you just wrote created a circular reference. To remove the message, select Cancel.

DISPLAYING THE CIRCULAR INDICATOR ON THE STATUS BAR

Excel's status bar will also indicate there is a circular reference by displaying the word "circular," sometimes followed by a cell reference. An example of this is shown below:

Ready		Circular: A2

Sometimes you may see the word "circular" in the status bar with no cell reference:

Ready		Circular

This indicates there is a circular reference in another sheet which could be in the same file or in a different file. The word "circular" with a cell reference indicates that the cell in question is at least partially responsible for the circular reference.

An essential check, which will help prevent unintentional circular references, is to check that the status bar is free of the circular message.

RETURNING AN UNEXPECTED ZERO

Another indicator of a circular reference is when a formula returns an unexpected zero value. When this happens, you will also see the word "circular" in the status bar.

The three warning signs outlined above are designed to protect you from building unintentional circular references into your model.

INTENTIONAL CIRCULAR REFERENCES

The most common intentional circular reference in a financial model is created by calculating interest using ending debt or cash balances. Interest expense flows through the cash flow statement and the cash flow statement determines the debt balance which determines interest expense. Likewise, interest income flows through the cash flow statement and the cash flow statement determines the cash balance which determines interest income. Some financial modelers avoid circular references by calculating interest on the previous year's cash or debt balances. However, as long as you adopt the procedures outlined below, intentional circular references can be a powerful addition to your financial models. If not properly managed, circular references can cause modeling nightmares!

ITERATION SETTING

Excel finds a solution to a circular problem through a process of iteration. In order for Excel to iterate and find a solution to a circular problem, you must activate the iteration setting in Tools, Options.

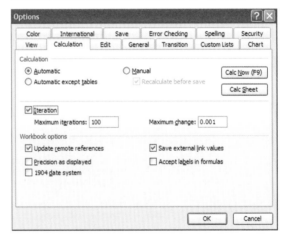

However, you will recall from the previous section that activating iteration can hide accidental circular references. Therefore, adding intentional circular references to your model should be one of the last steps of your modeling process. You should therefore only have iteration activated when reading the results of the model and not when building the model.

WORKING WITH INTENTIONAL CIRCULAR REFERENCES

Your model can be in one of two states: work-in-progress state or finished state. It will also flip between each state. For example, if you show a "finished" model to your MD, your MD may ask for a more detailed analysis of revenues. The model therefore flips back to "work-in-progress" state as you add the analysis!

Work-in-progress state

Your model is in work-in-progress when you are changing formulae and changing the model structure. When your model is in work-in-progress state, you should ensure that:

- There are no circular references
- Iteration is turned off

This will ensure that your model is protected from accidental circular references when you start working on the model.

You can remove the intentional circular references temporarily by deleting them and reinserting them later when you need them. An efficient way to do this is by COPYING the formula to the right hand side of the area you will delete them from. When you need to use them again, rather than rewriting the entire formula, you can simply COPY them back again. An example of this is shown below:

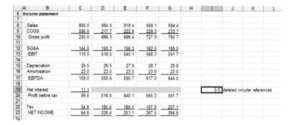

Finished state

Your model is in finished state when you are reading output from the model. Because the numbers need to be correct, you need to have:

- Intentional circular references linked into the model (e.g. the calculation of interest)
- Iteration activated

This will ensure your model iterates to find solutions to your intentional circular references.

Circular toggle

A circular toggle allows you to switch circular references on and off. It saves you from having to delete and reintroduce the formula creating the intentional circular when you want to switch between work-in-progress state and finished state. A circular toggle works by using a 1 or 0 switch cell and an IF function. The IF function returns the reference creating the circularity if the switch cell is equal to 1 and returns 0 if the switch cell is equal to 0.

An example of a circular toggle is shown in the following worksheet:

	D19		▼	f_x	=IF($I$19=1,D43,0)									
	A	B	C	D	E	F	G	H	I	J	K	L	M
11													
12	SG&A		144.5	150.3	156.3	162.5	169.0						
13	EBIT		110.5	516.0	540.1	565.3	591.7						
14													
15	Depreciation		25.5	26.5	27.6	28.7	29.8						
16	Amortisation		23.0	23.0	23.0	23.0	23.0						
17	EBITDA		159.0	565.6	590.7	617.0	644.5						
18													
19	Net interest		11.1	0.0	0.0	0.0	0.0		0.0	Circular Toggle (1 = circular; 0 = noncircular)			
20	Profit before tax		99.5	516.0	540.1	565.3	591.7						
21													
22	Tax		34.8	180.6	189.0	197.9	207.1						
23	NET INCOME		64.6	336.4	351.1	367.5	384.6						

Cell I19 is the switch cell. Cells D19:G19 contain the IF functions for each year of the analysis. In this example, the IF functions return net interest expense for each year (which are in cells D43:G43) when the 1 has been entered into the switch cell. They return a zero value when 0 has been entered into the switch cell. The zero value removes the circularity from the model.

Therefore, to put the model into work-in-progress state:

- Set the circular toggle switch to zero
- Deactivate iteration in Tools, Options

And to put the model into finished state:

- Set the circular toggle switch to 1
- Activate iteration in Tools, Options

The error state problem

It is very common for circular models to become infected with error values such as #REF, #VALUE, #NAME, and #DIV/0. This happens when the model is in finished state (i.e. the iteration setting is active and the model is iterating through intentional circulars) and the user creates an error. The error flows through to the circular cells and infects the model. Even when the user corrects the problem that caused the error in the first place, all circular cells in the model remain infected with an error value.

The error state problem is commonly referred to as the REF problem because many unseasoned modelers delete rows in their models without first putting the model into work-in-progress state. Any formulae referencing the cells in the deleted row would then return #REF. This error value would flow through the circular cells and infect the model.

A user typing text into an input cell that requires a value is another cause of the error state problem. Formulae dependent on that input cell would return the #VALUE error value, which would flow through to the circular cells and infect the model with #VALUE errors.

One way to reduce the risk of this "infection" happening is to remove circular references from your model while you are changing the structure of the model. In other words, as mentioned in the previous section, always put the model into work-in-progress state when you are changing the structure of the model.

If, however, you are reading output from the model (the model is therefore in finished state) and you enter text into an input cell that

should contain a value, the model will get infected with #VALUE errors. To correct this situation:

1. **Correct the initial problem.** For example, if you entered text into an input cell that should contain a number, enter the correct number into the input cell. Or, if you deleted a row, fix all the formulae that refer to that row.

2. **Remove the circular references from the model.** Either delete them using the DELETE key or, if you have one, set your circular toggle to zero.

3. **Reintroduce the circular references into the model.** Either undo the delete using CTRL + Z or set the circular toggle back to 1.

As you can see, this is another benefit of building a toggle switch into a circular model. It makes correcting the error state problem nice and easy. However, remember, for this to work **you must correct the problem that caused the error state in the first place.**

Super Flexible Output Tables

INTRODUCTION

An important part of your modeling toolkit is the ability to extract information from your models and present it in an output table. The output table should be flexible so that when the assumptions of your model change, the output table will update. Furthermore, a flexible output table will also allow you to easily specify which line items to extract from the model without having to rewrite formulae. You can extract information from your model by using Excel's lookup functions.

LOOKUP FUNCTIONS

A lookup function essentially returns a value from a table by looking up another value. A telephone directory provides a good analogy. If you want to find a person's telephone number, you first locate the name and then retrieve the corresponding number.

There are a number of functions you can use to look up information in your model. This chapter will focus on the following functions:

- VLOOKUP
- HLOOKUP
- INDEX
- MATCH

VLOOKUP FUNCTION

The VLOOKUP function looks for a value you specify in the first column of a lookup table and returns the corresponding value in a specified table column. VLOOKUP stands for vertical lookup; this lookup function finds information in a vertical list. The syntax of the VLOOKUP function is:

=*VLOOKUP(**lookup_value**,**table_array**,**col_index_num**,**range_lookup**)*

lookup_value   The value to be looked up in the first column of the lookup table.

table_array   The range that contains the lookup table.

col_index_num   The column number within the table from which the corresponding matching value will be returned.

range_lookup   This is an optional argument. If TRUE or omitted, an approximate match is returned (if an exact match is not found, the next largest value that is less than lookup_value is returned). If FALSE, VLOOKUP will search for an exact match (if VLOOKUP can not find an exact match, it returns the #N/A error value).

Note: If range_lookup is TRUE or omitted, the first column of the table_array must be in ascending order. If lookup_value is smaller than the smallest value in the table_array, VLOOKUP returns the

#'N/A error value. If range_lookup is FALSE, the first column of the table_array need not be in ascending order.

Lookup values

A classic example of the VLOOKUP formula involves a sales commission table which shows the commission rate on a given level of sales. The VLOOKUP function can be used to return the commission rate for a specified level of sales.

In the worksheet extract below, cell C4 returns the commission rate based on the sales amount input in cell C3. Cell C4 contains the following formula:

```
=VLOOKUP(C3,B9:D14,3)
```

	A	B	C	D
1		*Assumptions*		
2				
3		Sales amount	120,000.0	
4		Commission	2.0%	
5				
6		*Commision table*		
7				
8		Sales is greater than or equal to...	But less than...	Commision rate
9		0.0	25,000.0	0.0%
10		25,001.0	50,000.0	1.0%
11		50,001.0	100,000.0	1.5%
12		100,001.0	150,000.0	2.0%
13		150,001.0	200,000.0	2.5%
14		200,000.0		3.0%

Excel is looking for the lookup value in cell C3 in the first column of the table array B9:D14. Because the range argument has been omitted, an exact match is not required. If an exact match is not found, the VLOOKUP function finds the next largest value that is less than lookup_value and returns the information in the column specified by column_index_number, which in this case is 3. Column 3 in the table array contains the commission rate. For the above example to work, the first column in the table array must be in ascending order. This is because the range_lookup argument is omitted.

Lookup text

In the commission table example above, the VLOOKUP function looked for a value and returned information from the corresponding specified column. In other words, the lookup value was a value and therefore the first column in the table array contained values. The next example is an example of VLOOKUP looking up text.

The worksheet extract below has a table of earnings information for a number of different businesses. Cell C3 contains the lookup value, which is a company name. Cell C4 contains the following VLOOKUP formula, which returns EBIT for the specified company:

`=VLOOKUP(C3,B10:E14,3,FALSE)`

	A	B	C	D	E	F
1		*Assumptions*				
2						
3		Company name:	Holst			
4		EBIT:	70.0			
5						
6						
7		*Data*				
8						
9		**Company name**	**EBIT**	**EBITDA**	**Net Income**	
10		Crash	100.0	120.0	50.0	
11		Fire	243.0	289.0	121.5	
12		Holst	50.0	70.0	25.0	
13		Tunde	23.0	50.0	11.5	
14		Jolst	(12.0)	4.0	(18.0)	
15						

Excel is looking for the lookup value in C3 in the first column of the table array B10:E14. Because the range argument is FALSE, an exact match is required and the company names in the table array do not need to be in ascending order. In this case, the VLOOKUP function finds the lookup value "Holst" in the first column of the table array and returns the corresponding information from column 3. If a company name was entered that did not match any company name in the table, the VLOOKUP function would return #N/A.

HLOOKUP FUNCTION

The HLOOKUP function works just like the VLOOKUP function, but table_array is arranged horizontally. The HLOOKUP function looks for lookup_value in the first row of table_array and returns the corresponding value in the specified table row. The syntax for the HLOOKUP function is as follows:

*=HLOOKUP(**lookup_value**,**table_array**,**row_index_num**,**range_lookup**)*

lookup_value	The value to be looked up in the first row of the lookup table.
table_array	The range that contains the lookup table.
row_index_num	The row number within the table from which the corresponding matching value is returned.
range_lookup	This is an optional argument. If TRUE or omitted, an approximate match is returned (if an exact match is not found, the next largest value that is less than lookup_value is returned). If FALSE, HLOOKUP will search for an exact match (if HLOOKUP can

not find an exact match, it returns the #N/A error value).

The worksheet extract below shows the commission example with a horizontal lookup:

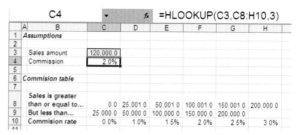

	C4		▾		fx	=HLOOKUP(C3,C8:H10,3)	

	B	C	D	E	F	G	H
1	*Assumptions*						
2							
3	Sales amount	120,000.0					
4	Commission	2.0%					
5							
6	*Commision table*						
7							
8	Sales is greater than or equal to...	0.0	25,001.0	50,001.0	100,001.0	150,001.0	200,000.0
9	But less than...	25,000.0	50,000.0	100,000.0	150,000.0	200,000.0	
10	Commision rate	0.0%	1.0%	1.5%	2.0%	2.5%	3.0%

Excel is looking for the lookup value in cell C3 in the first row of the table array C8:H10. Because range_lookup has been omitted, an exact match is not required. In this example, HLOOKUP returns the commission rate 2.0% which is in the 3rd row of the table array.

INDEX FUNCTION

The INDEX functions returns the contents of a cell from a specified range. The syntax for the INDEX function is:

=INDEX(array,row_num,column_num)

array   A range of cells. If array contains only one row or column, the corresponding row_num or column_num argument is optional.

row_num   A row within the array.

column_num A column within the array.

The table in the worksheet extract below shows a business's sales figures by quarter and region. The INDEX function in cell C6 returns the Asia sales figure for quarter 4.

	C6		▾		fx	=INDEX(C10:G13,C3,C4

	B	C	D	E	F	G	H
1	*Assumptions*						
2							
3	Row:	3.0					
4	Column:	4.0					
5							
6	Sales	1,188.0					
7							
8	*Table*						
9		Q1	Q2	Q3	Q4	Total	
10	Americas	1,155.0	1,577.9	1,815.5	1,930.5	6,478.9	
11	EMEA	1,386.0	1,213.7	1,396.6	1,485.0	5,481.3	
12	Asia	808.5	971.0	1,117.2	1,188.0	4,084.7	
13	Total	3,349.5	3,762.6	4,329.3	4,603.5	16,044.9	

This is because the row argument input in cell C3 is 3, the column argument input in cell C4 is 4, and the array is C10:G13. The Asia

sales figure is the value 1,188.0 in the 3rd row and 4th column of the array C10:G13.

MATCH FUNCTION

The MATCH function returns the relative position of an item in an array that matches a specified value. It is very powerful when used in conjunction with the VLOOKUP and INDEX functions explained above. The MATCH function has the following syntax:

*=MATCH(**lookup_value,lookup_array,match_type**)*

lookup_value   The value you want to match in the lookup array.

lookup_array   A contiguous range of cells containing possible lookup values.

match_type   The number -1, 0, or 1. Match_type specifies how Excel matches lookup_value with values in lookup_array. This guide uses the 0 argument, which finds an exact match. Refer to Excel's online help on the MATCH function for an explanation of the -1 and 1 values in match_type.

Cells B10:B13 in the worksheet extract below contain the regions from the previous INDEX function example.

	A	B	C	D
1		*Assumptions*		
2				
3		Region	EMEA	
4		MATCH	2.0	
5				
6				
7				
8		*Table*		
9				
10		Americas		
11		EMEA		
12		Asia		
13		Total		
14				

Cell C3 contains lookup_value, which is EMEA in this example. Cell C4 contains the MATCH function which has been written as:

```
=MATCH(C3,B10:B13,0)
```

The MATCH function returns the number 2 because EMEA (the lookup value) is the second item in the array B10:B13. The match_type argument has been entered as 0 so that MATCH finds an exact match in the array. If your lookup value does not match any of the items in the array, the MATCH function returns #N/A.

The MATCH array can also be horizontal. Cells C9:G9 in the worksheet extract below contain the quarter headings from the sales commission example above. The following MATCH formula is in cell C6:

```
=MATCH(C5,C9:G9,0)
```

The lookup value Q3 is in cell C5. In this example, the MATCH function returns the number 3 because Q3 is the third item in the array C9:G9. As with the previous MATCH example, the match type is 0 so that MATCH finds an exact match.

A	B	C	D	E	F	G	H
1	Assumptions						
2							
3	Region	EMEA					
4	MATCH	2.0					
5	Quarter	Q3					
6	MATCH	3.0					
7							
8	Table						
9		Q1	Q2	Q3	Q4	Total	
10	Americas						
11	EMEA						
12	Asia						
13	Total						

MATCH USED IN CONJUNCTION WITH INDEX

The MATCH function used in conjunction with the INDEX function is a very powerful lookup tool. If you substitute the MATCH function into the row and column arguments of the INDEX function, you can enter text as lookup values to extract information from a range. An example will help illustrate this concept.

In the worksheet extract below, cell C5 contains the following INDEX with an embedded MATCH formula:

```
=INDEX(C10:G13,MATCH(C3,B10:B13,0),MATCH(C4,C9:G9,
0))
```

A	B	C	D	E	F	G	
1	Assumptions						
2							
3	Region	EMEA					
4	Quarter	Q3					
5	Sales	1,396.6					
6							
7							
8	Table						
9		Q1	Q2	Q3	Q4	Total	
10	Americas	1,155.0	1,577.9	1,815.5	1,930.5	6,478.9	
11	EMEA	1,386.0	1,213.7	1,396.6	1,485.0	5,481.3	
12	Asia	808.5	971.0	1,117.2	1,188.0	4,084.7	
13	Total	3,349.5	3,762.6	4,329.3	4,603.5	16,044.9	

Range C10:G13 represents the array for the INDEX function. The first MATCH function returns the row argument for the INDEX

function, which in this example is 2. The second MATCH function returns the column argument for the INDEX function, which in this case is 3. Therefore, the INDEX function returns the sales for EMEA in Q3 (the value 1,396.6 in cell E11).

MATCH USED IN CONJUNCTION WITH **VLOOKUP** AND **HLOOKUP**

MATCH used in conjunction with VLOOKUP and HLOOKUP functions can also be powerful. The MATCH function is simply substituted into the col_index_num and row_index_num arguments of these two functions.

In the worksheet extract below, the following VLOOKUP function is being used to return the EBITDA for the company named Holst.

```
=VLOOKUP(C3,B11:E15,MATCH(C4,B10:E10,0),FALSE)
```

	A	B	C	D	E
1		*Assumptions*			
2					
3		Company name:	Holst		
4		Information	EBITDA		
5		VLOOKUP:	70.0		
6					
7					
8		*Data*			
9					
10		Company name	EBIT	EBITDA	Net Income
11		Crash	100.0	120.0	50.0
12		Fire	243.0	289.0	121.5
13		Holst	50.0	70.0	25.0
14		Tunde	23.0	50.0	11.5
15		Jolst	(12.0)	4.0	(18.0)
16					

As you see, the MATCH function has been substituted into the col_index_num argument of VLOOKUP. This means that you can use text to specify the column from which Excel returns information. The MATCH function uses this text to return the relevant col_index_num for VLOOKUP.

Grand Scenarios

INTRODUCTION

The ability to add scenarios to your model and control these
scenarios quickly and easily is a valuable part of your financial
modeling toolkit. This chapter will focus on the key "switch" functions
you will need to use to switch scenarios in your models. We will then
look at different options available to control these functions. As you
switch scenarios and methodologies, you will also want your
footnotes and headings to update automatically. We will therefore
address various text functions for doing so.

SWITCH FUNCTIONS

Switch functions allow you to switch between different scenarios and
methodologies in financial models. For example, switch functions
can be used to quickly and easily switch between different growth
rate scenarios. Or a switch function could be used to activate and
deactivate a mid-year adjustment convention in a discounted cash
flow model. There are many functions in Excel you can use for this
purpose. This guide will focus on three functions:

- CHOOSE
- OFFSET
- MATCH

CHOOSE FUNCTION

The CHOOSE function uses an index number to return a value from
a list of value arguments. You can use the CHOOSE function to
store and return up to 29 values. The CHOOSE function has the
following syntax:

*=CHOOSE(**index_num**,**value1**,value2,value3,......)*

Cells A1:A7 in the worksheet below contain the days of the week.
Cell A10 contains the number 4, which will be the index number of
the CHOOSE function.

	A	B	
1	Monday		
2	Tuesday		
3	Wednesday		
4	Thursday		
5	Friday		
6	Saturday		
7	Sunday		
8			
9			
10	4.0	Thursday	
11			

Cell B10 contains the CHOOSE function, which has been written as:

```
=CHOOSE(A10,A1,A2,A3,A4,A5,A6,A7)
```

In this example the CHOOSE function returns Thursday because Cell A4 is the fourth reference in the CHOOSE function and contains the word "Thursday". When you change the index number, the CHOOSE function will return the value that corresponds to the index number in question. In this example, if you change the index number to 2, the CHOOSE function returns Tuesday.

Modeling application

The CHOOSE function is commonly used to switch scenarios in financial models. The worksheet below contains three sales growth scenarios in rows 6 to 8: base, best, and worst respectively. Cell C4 contains index number 1. Cells D10:H10 contain a CHOOSE function.

A	B	C	D	E	F	G	H
1	Assumptions	Year 0	Year 1	Year 2	Year 3	Year 4	Year 5
2							
3	Sales growth scenarios:						
4	Scenario number	1.0					
5							
6	Base		4.0%	4.0%	4.0%	4.0%	4.0%
7	Best		10.0%	10.0%	10.0%	10.0%	10.0%
8	Worst		1.0%	1.0%	1.0%	1.0%	1.0%
9							
10	Sales growth		4.0%	4.0%	4.0%	4.0%	4.0%

The CHOOSE function has been entered into cell D10 as:

```
=CHOOSE($C$4,D6,D7,D8)
```

TIP!

Absolute Referencing
To lock a reference in a formula or function when copying across, press **F4** when referencing the cell as you write the formula or function.

Cell C4 is the index number, which has been absolute referenced for when the formula is copied across to column H. Cells D6, D7 and D8 are the growth rates of the base case, best case, and worst case scenarios respectively. These are relative references so that when the formula is copied across to column H the cells containing growth rates for the relevant years are picked up. Entering 1 as the index number in cell C4 will return the base case growth rates, entering 2 as the index number will return the best case growth rates, and entering index number 3 will return the worst case growth rates. Entering an index number where no value exists (e.g. 4) will return a #VALUE error. The sales growth line in row 10 can now be used as the sales growth assumption for a model as shown below:

D14		f_x	=C14*(1+D10)				
A	B	C	D	E	F	G	H
1	Assumptions	Year 0	Year 1	Year 2	Year 3	Year 4	Year 5
2							
3	Sales growth scenarios:						
4	Scenario number	1.0					
5							
6	Base		4.0%	4.0%	4.0%	4.0%	4.0%
7	Best		10.0%	10.0%	10.0%	10.0%	10.0%
8	Worst		1.0%	1.0%	1.0%	1.0%	1.0%
9							
10	Sales growth		4.0%	4.0%	4.0%	4.0%	4.0%
11							
12	Income statement						
13							
14	Sales	850.0	884.0	919.4	956.1	994.4	1,034.2
15							

OFFSET FUNCTION

In its most basic form, the OFFSET function returns the contents of a cell that is a specified number of rows and columns from a specified cell. The syntax of the OFFSET function is:

=OFFSET(reference,row,column)

reference	The cell reference from which you want to base the OFFSET function. This is referred to as the starting point or reference point.
row	The number of rows up or down from the reference cell you want OFFSET to refer to. The row argument can be a positive number to go down or negative number to go up from the reference point.
column	The number of cells left or right from the reference cell you want OFFSET to refer to. The column index number can be positive to go right or negative to go left from the reference point.

Note: There are two additional optional arguments: height and width. These will be explored in the section on dynamic range names on page 54 of this guide.

Cells A1:C7 in the worksheet extract below contain names, except cell B4. Cell B9 contains the number 3 which represents the row argument. Cell B10 contains the number 1 which represents the column argument. And cell B12 contains the OFFSET function.

	A	B	C
1	Alastair	Justin	Rahul
2	James	Roman	Richard
3	Stefano	Karen	Tunde
4	Mary		Alison
5	Aasha	John	Norman
6	Katie	Colin	Kathleen
7	Jean	Andrea	Ed
8			
9	Row	3.0	
10	Column	1.0	
11			
12	OFFSET	Ed	

The OFFSET function in cell B12 has been written as:

```
=OFFSET(B4,B9,B10)
```

In this example, cell B4 is the reference cell or starting point. The OFFSET function is therefore returning the contents of the cell which is 3 rows down and 1 column over from the starting point. This is cell C7, which contains the text "Ed".

With the example above, if you change the row argument to -3 and -1, the OFFSET function would return the contents of cell A1 which is the text "Alastair". This is because cell A1 is three rows up and one column left from the starting point.

If you type a row or column coordinate that relates to a non-existent cell reference, OFFSET returns a #REF error. For example, using the illustration above, if you specified -10 as the row argument, assuming the starting point is still B4, this would return a #REF because the implied cell does not exist.

Modeling application

The OFFSET function provides a clever way of switching between scenarios. As with the previous CHOOSE modeling application, the worksheet below contains three sales growth scenarios in rows 6 to 8: base, best, and worst. Cell C4 contains index number 1. This time, each column in row 10 contains an OFFSET function.

| D10 | | ▾ | f_x | =OFFSET(D5,$C$4,0) | | | |

	A	B	C	D	E	F	G	H
1		Assumptions		Year 0	Year 1	Year 2	Year 3	Year 4	Year 5
2								
3		Sales growth scenarios:						
4		Scenario number	1.0					
5								
6		Base		4.0%	4.0%	4.0%	4.0%	4.0%
7		Best		10.0%	10.0%	10.0%	10.0%	10.0%
8		Worst		1.0%	1.0%	1.0%	1.0%	1.0%
9								
10		Sales growth		4.0%	4.0%	4.0%	4.0%	4.0%
11								

The OFFSET function has been entered into cell D10 and then copied across. In cell D10, it has been entered as:

```
=OFFSET(D5,$C$4,0)
```

Cell D5 is the starting point. This is a relative cell address so that the reference point adjusts to the relevant year. Cell C4 is the row coordinate, which is absolute. The column argument is 0 as this is "one dimensional" OFFSET. It simply returns the contents of a cell a specified number of rows DOWN from the reference point for a given year. In the above example, the row argument is 1 and for year 1 the reference cell is D5. In other words, the OFFSET function returns the contents of cell D6, which is one row down from the reference point. When copying the formula across to year 2, the row argument is still C4 (because it is absolute), but the reference point now becomes E5. Therefore, for year 2, the OFFSET function returns the contents of cell E6, which is one cell down from the reference point.

The advantage of using OFFSET in this modeling application is that you can add more scenarios or cases without having to adjust the OFFSET function, as long as you add the case under the previous case as shown below:

	A	B	C	D	E	F	G	H
1		Assumptions		Year 0	Year 1	Year 2	Year 3	Year 4	Year 5
2								
3		Sales growth scenarios:						
4		Scenario number	1.0					
5								
6		Base		4.0%	4.0%	4.0%	4.0%	4.0%
7		Best		10.0%	10.0%	10.0%	10.0%	10.0%
8		Worst		1.0%	1.0%	1.0%	1.0%	1.0%
9		Another case		12.0%	12.0%	12.0%	12.0%	12.0%
10								
11		Sales growth		4.0%	4.0%	4.0%	4.0%	4.0%
12								

If you use the CHOOSE function, you would have to add the new case to the function as an additional value argument.

Once again, when using OFFSET, the sales growth line in row 11 can now be used as the sales growth assumption for a model as shown below:

D15		▾	ƒx	=C15*(1+D11)			
	A B	C	D	E	F	G	H
1	**Assumptions**	Year 0	Year 1	Year 2	Year 3	Year 4	Year 5
2							
3	Sales growth scenarios:						
4	Scenario number	1.0					
5							
6	Base		4.0%	4.0%	4.0%	4.0%	4.0%
7	Best		10.0%	10.0%	10.0%	10.0%	10.0%
8	Worst		1.0%	1.0%	1.0%	1.0%	1.0%
9	Another case		12.0%	12.0%	12.0%	12.0%	12.0%
10							
11	Sales growth		4.0%	4.0%	4.0%	4.0%	4.0%
12							
13	*Income statement*						
14							
15	Sales	850.0	884.0	919.4	956.1	994.4	1,034.2
16							

MATCH FUNCTION

The MATCH function returns the relative position of an item in an array that matches a specified value. It has the following syntax:

=MATCH(lookup_value,lookup_array,match_type)

lookup_value   The value you want to match in the lookup array.

lookup_array   A contiguous range of cells containing possible lookup values.

match_type   The number -1, 0, or 1. Match_type specifies how Excel matches lookup_value with values in lookup_array. This guide uses the 0 argument, which finds an exact match. Refer to Excel's online help on the MATCH function for an explanation of the -1 and 1 values in match_type.

Cells A1:A7 in the worksheet extract below contain 7 names. Cell A10 contains the text "Kylie", which will be referenced as the lookup value in the MATCH function.

	A	B	C
1	Gloria		
2	Wayne		
3	Kylie		
4	Tina		
5	Lola		
6	Britney		
7	Whitney		
8			
9			
10	Kylie	3.0	
11			

Cell B10 contains a MATCH function which is returning value 3. It has been entered as:

```
=MATCH(A10,A1:A7,0)
```

In this example, the MATCH function returns 3 because the lookup value in A10 ("Kylie") is the third item in the lookup array, A1:A7. The match_type argument has been entered as 0, so that MATCH finds an exact match in the array. If your lookup_value does not match any of the items in the array, the MATCH function returns an #N/A error as shown below.

	A	B	C
1	Gloria		
2	Wayne		
3	Kylie		
4	Tina		
5	Lola		
6	Britney		
7	Whitney		
8			
9			
10	Beckham	#N/A	
11			

Modeling application

The MATCH function can be used in conjunction with the CHOOSE or OFFSET functions explained above. The MATCH function can be substituted in the index_number argument of CHOOSE and the row or column arguments of OFFSET. The examples below will help illustrate this concept.

MATCH in conjunction with CHOOSE

In the sales scenario modeling application presented above, you would switch scenarios by typing an index number from 1 to 3 in cell C4. Using the MATCH function in conjunction with the CHOOSE function would allow you to type the case name you want to see. For example, if you want to see the base case, you would be able to type the word "base" instead of the number 1. To see the best case, you would be able to type the word "best" instead of the number 2, and so on. This is illustrated below.

	B	C	D	E	F	G	H
1	Assumptions	Year 0	Year 1	Year 2	Year 3	Year 4	Year 5
2							
3	Sales growth scenarios:						
4	Scenario number	Best					
5							
6	Base		4.0%	4.0%	4.0%	4.0%	4.0%
7	Best		10.0%	10.0%	10.0%	10.0%	10.0%
8	Worst		1.0%	1.0%	1.0%	1.0%	1.0%
9							
10	Sales growth		10.0%	10.0%	10.0%	10.0%	10.0%
11							

The CHOOSE and MATCH functions have been written in cell D10 as follows:

```
=CHOOSE(MATCH($C$4,$B$6:$B$8,0),D6,D7,D8)
```

As you can see, the MATCH function has been substituted into the index_number argument of the CHOOSE function. Cell C4 now contains the lookup value for the MATCH function. The lookup array of the MATCH function is range B6:B9. So in this example, the MATCH function returns the number 2 as lookup_value and "best" is the second item in the lookup array. The CHOOSE function therefore returns the "best" sales growth rate because this is the second of the CHOOSE values. Finally, the formula has been copied across to cell H10.

If you input text that MATCH can not find in the lookup array, the CHOOSE function will return an #N/A error.

MATCH in conjunction with OFFSET
In the sales scenario modeling application presented above, you would switch scenarios by inputting an index number from 1 to 3 in cell C4. Using the MATCH function in conjunction with the OFFSET function would allow you to type the case name you want to see as described in the *MATCH in conjunction with CHOOSE* application presented above. In this application, you would substitute the MATCH function into the row argument as shown below:

	B	C	D	E	F	G	H
1	*Assumptions*	Year 0	Year 1	Year 2	Year 3	Year 4	Year 5
2							
3	*Sales growth scenarios:*						
4	Scenario number	Best					
5							
6	Base		4.0%	4.0%	4.0%	4.0%	4.0%
7	Best		10.0%	10.0%	10.0%	10.0%	10.0%
8	Worst		1.0%	1.0%	1.0%	1.0%	1.0%
9							
10	Sales growth		10.0%	10.0%	10.0%	10.0%	10.0%

In the worksheet extract above, cell D10 contains the following formula:

```
=OFFSET(D5,MATCH($C$4,$B$6:$B$8,0),0)
```

Once again, in the example above the MATCH function is returning a 2 as the lookup value because "best" is the second item in the lookup array. The MATCH function has been substituted into the row argument of the OFFSET function. The OFFSET function is therefore returning the "best" growth rate assumptions because these assumptions are 2 rows down from the relevant starting point in row 5 of each year.

If you input text that MATCH can not find in the lookup array, the OFFSET function will return an #N/A error.

CONTROLS

Some financial modelers add controls to their worksheets to make their models more user-friendly. For example, being able to select an option such as "Best Case" from a drop down box is more user-friendly than typing in a number assigned to that case. Furthermore, controls act as input masks. Rather than giving your user free rein to type any number to select a scenario, controls limit your user's options. This is a particularly useful feature because switches can return error values if the correct number is not entered and error values can infect circular models.

USING LIST DATA VALIDATION

With list data validation, you can control what your user types into a cell. This is very useful in the context of the previous two modeling applications. In these modeling applications, the user must correctly type one of the available cases (base, best, or worst) or the functions will return #N/A errors. For example, if your user misspells the word "best," the #N/A error will appear. If you have a circular model, this error can infect the entire model with error values which can be difficult for the novice user to remove. List data validation solves this problem because your users will have to choose a case from a list.

To install data validation in the context of the previous modeling applications:

1. Select the lookup cell. In the example below, this is cell C4.

2. Choose Data, Validation from the menu. The Data Validation dialog box will appear.

3. Choose List from the Allow drop down box.

4. Select the Source box and select the items to appear in the list. In this example, these are the case names in cells B6:B9.

Validation criteria

Allow:

List

☑ Ignore blank

Data:

between

☑ In-cell dropdown

Source:

=$B$6:$B$9

5. Choose OK to close the Data Validation dialog box.

Now that you have applied data validation to the cell, the cell is active and a drop down box will appear as shown below.

Sales growth scenarios:
Case: Base

You can now select the different cases using the drop down box. You can click the drop down box with the mouse. Or when the cell is active, hold down ALT and use the down arrow key to activate the drop down box. Use the arrow keys to select the desired case, followed by ENTER.

ON-SHEET CONTROLS

On-sheet controls provide another way to control a switch. To use the on-sheet controls, you must display the Forms toolbar. To do so, choose View, Toolbars, Forms from the menu.

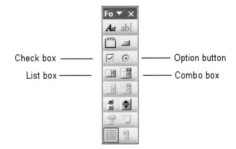

Check box ————— ☑ ◉ ————— Option button
List box ————— ▣ ▣ ————— Combo box

This section will address four on-sheet controls:

- Option button
- Combo box
- List box
- Check box

Working with controls

Before we address the specific functionality of each control, there is some general information you need to know. This section will focus on:

- Creating a control
- Selecting a control
- Sizing a control
- Copying a control
- Moving a control
- Deleting a control
- Linking a control
- Aligning controls

Creating a control

To add an on-sheet control to your worksheet:

1. Select the desired control button on the Forms toolbar. As you point to the worksheet area your mouse pointer will turn into a crosshair symbol [+].

2. Click and drag on the worksheet to create the control.

3. Click away from the control to deselect it.

Selecting a control

To select a control or a number of controls hold down the CTRL key and click the control or controls with the mouse. As shown below, a placeholder line will appear around the control to indicate that it is selected.

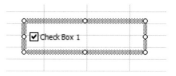

Sizing a control

To size a control, select the control and click and drag one of the round grab handles. The illustration below points to the bottom middle grab handle of a check box. As you can see, there are 8 grab handles in total.

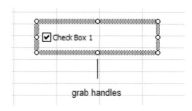

Copying a control

To copy a control, select the control, hold down the CTRL key, and drag the control from its placeholder line. Release the mouse before you release the CTRL key.

Moving a control

To move a control, either:

- Select the control and drag it from the placeholder line
- Select the control and use the arrow keys to move the control in the desired direction

Deleting a control

To delete a control, select the control and press the DELETE key on your keyboard.

Linking a control

In order for controls to work, you must link them to a cell. The control will return a value in the linked cell which can then be used in a switch function, such as CHOOSE or OFFSET. When you select one of the items from a control, this determines the cell link value. This will be discussed in more detail in subsequent sections. To link a control to a cell:

1. Right click the control.

2. Choose Format Control. The Format Control dialog box will appear.

3. Select the Control tab.

4. Select the Cell link field and select the cell you wish to link the control to.

It is a good idea to have a separate hidden sheet for all your cell link values so they are not visible.

Aligning controls

In order to align your controls with each other, you should use the align feature on the Drawing toolbar. If you try and align controls manually, they will not look aligned when you print the worksheet, even though they may look aligned on your screen.

To align your controls:

1. Select the controls you wish to align.

2. Insert the Drawing toolbar by choosing View, Toolbars, Drawing from the menu.

3. Select the Draw button on the Drawing toolbar and choose Align or Distribute.

4. Select the desired option under Align or Distribute.

The controls

Option buttons

Option buttons must exist as a group. They act like old fashioned radio buttons: when you press one button the other pops up.

Once you create an option button you can change its text by selecting the option button and clicking on the text.

The worksheet extract below contains three option buttons that have been aligned horizontally and distributed vertically using the Align or Distribute option from the Drawing toolbar.

These option buttons are useless unless they are linked to a cell. To link them to a cell, right click on any one option button and follow the cell link procedure explained in the *Linking a control* section above.

In the following example, the option buttons have been linked to cell B7.

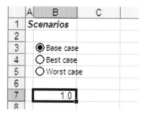

The cell link value is 1 because the first option button is selected. If the second option button were selected, the cell link value would be 2; if the third option button were selected, the cell link value would be 3. The cell link value assigned to an option button depends on the order the option button was created in. In the example above, the base case option button was created first, followed by the best case, and then the worst case.

The cell link value can now be used as an input for a switch function such as CHOOSE or OFFSET. In the example below, the cell link value is used as the index_number argument for the CHOOSE function.

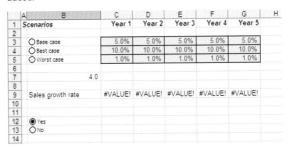

C9	▼	fx	=CHOOSE($B$7,C3,C4,C5)				
	A	B	C	D	E	F	G	H

	A	B	C	D	E	F	G	H
1		Scenarios	Year 1	Year 2	Year 3	Year 4	Year 5	
2								
3	◉	Base case	5.0%	5.0%	5.0%	5.0%	5.0%	
4	○	Best case	10.0%	10.0%	10.0%	10.0%	10.0%	
5	○	Worst case	1.0%	1.0%	1.0%	1.0%	1.0%	
6								
7		1.0						
8								
9		Sales growth rate	5.0%	5.0%	5.0%	5.0%	5.0%	

When an option button is selected, the cell link value changes, and the CHOOSE function returns the appropriate value. As mentioned in the section on cell links, you may wish to put the cell link value on a separate sheet to keep it out of the way.

If you are going to use more than one set of option buttons you must group each set for each group to work independently. An example will help illustrate this.

In the worksheet below another group of option buttons has been added.

	A	B	C	D	E	F	G	H
1		Scenarios	Year 1	Year 2	Year 3	Year 4	Year 5	
2								
3	○	Base case	5.0%	5.0%	5.0%	5.0%	5.0%	
4	○	Best case	10.0%	10.0%	10.0%	10.0%	10.0%	
5	○	Worst case	1.0%	1.0%	1.0%	1.0%	1.0%	
6								
7		4.0						
8								
9		Sales growth rate	#VALUE!	#VALUE!	#VALUE!	#VALUE!	#VALUE!	
10								
11								
12	◉	Yes						
13	○	No						
14								

Notice that the "Yes" option button is selected and the cell link in B7 returns 4. This is because the "Yes" button was the fourth button created and the two option button groups are not yet working independently. To solve this problem, you simple draw a group box button around each option button group. To do this:

1. Select the Group Box button ⬚ from the Forms toolbar.

2. Click and drag around a group of option buttons ensuring that the placeholders of all the buttons are inside the group box.

3. Change the group box text

In the example below, both groups of option buttons have been grouped. Furthermore, the second set of buttons has been cell linked to cell B16.

	A	B	C	D	E	F	G
1		Scenarios	Year 1	Year 2	Year 3	Year 4	Year 5
2		┌ Sale Growth					
3		○ Base case	5.0%	5.0%	5.0%	5.0%	5.0%
4		○ Best case	10.0%	10.0%	10.0%	10.0%	10.0%
5		◉ Worst case	1.0%	1.0%	1.0%	1.0%	1.0%
6							
7		3.0					
8							
9		Sales growth rate	1.0%	1.0%	1.0%	1.0%	1.0%
10							
11		┌ Mid-year discounting ──					
12		○ Yes					
13		◉ No					
14							
15							
16		2.0					

Combo box

The combo box on-sheet control is a drop down box. The user simply selects one of the options from the drop down box. As with all on-sheet controls you must specify a cell link. With the combo box, you must also specify an input range. The input range you specify should contain the items you want to see in the combo box. To specify the input range:

1. Enter the combo box items into a vertical contiguous set of cells. For example:

    Base case
    Best case
    Worst case

2. Create the combo box.

3. Right click the combo box and choose Format Control.

4. Select the Control tab.

5. Select the Input range field and select the cells containing the input range.

6. Choose OK.

In the example below the cell link of the combo box is B9 and the input range of the combo box is B5:B7. The CHOOSE functions in cells C11:G11 return the corresponding sales growth rates. To use the combo box, one would simply click the arrow and select the appropriate option.

| C11 | ▼ | f_x | =CHOOSE($B$9,C5,C6,C7) | | | | |

	A B	C	D	E	F	G	H
1	*Scenarios*	Year 1	Year 2	Year 3	Year 4	Year 5	
2							
3	Base case ▼						
4							
5	Base case	5.0%	5.0%	5.0%	5.0%	5.0%	
6	Best case	10.0%	10.0%	10.0%	10.0%	10.0%	
7	Worst case	1.0%	1.0%	1.0%	1.0%	1.0%	
8							
9	1.0						
10							
11	Sales growth rate	5.0%	5.0%	5.0%	5.0%	5.0%	
12							
13							

List box

The list box is almost identical to the combo box. The difference relates to the presentation of options. The list box displays the items without the user having to click a drop down arrow.

The example below shows a list box in action. The input range is B4:B6 and is hidden behind the list box. The cell link is B8. Once again, the CHOOSE functions in C10:G10 return the corresponding sales growth rates.

	A B	C	D	E	F	G
1	*Scenarios*	Year 1	Year 2	Year 3	Year 4	Year 5
2						
3						
4	Base case ▲	5.0%	5.0%	5.0%	5.0%	5.0%
5	Best case	10.0%	10.0%	10.0%	10.0%	10.0%
6	Worst case ▼	1.0%	1.0%	1.0%	1.0%	1.0%
7						
8	3.0					
9						
10	Sales growth rate	1.0%	1.0%	1.0%	1.0%	1.0%
11						

Check box

The check box gives you the ability to switch on or off an assumption or methodology in your model. A suitable analogy for a check box is a light switch, which gives you the ability to switch on and off a light.

The cell link of the check box returns TRUE when the box is checked or FALSE when the box is not checked. TRUE and FALSE are binomial operators. TRUE and 1 are equal values. FALSE and 0 are equal values.

In the example below, the check box is used in connection with an IF function. The cell link is I19. When the check box is checked, interest is shown and the model becomes circular. When the check box is not checked, the IF function returns zero and the model is not circular.

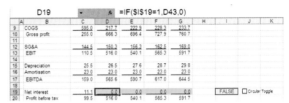

	A	B	C	D	E	F	G	H	I	J	K
9		COGS	595.0	217.7	222.9	228.3	233.7				
10		Gross profit	255.0	666.3	696.4	727.9	760.7				
11											
12		SG&A	144.5	150.3	156.3	162.5	169.0				
13		EBIT	110.5	516.0	540.1	565.3	591.7				
14											
15		Depreciation	25.5	26.5	27.6	26.7	29.8				
16		Amortisation	23.0	23.0	23.0	23.0	23.0				
17		EBITDA	159.0	565.6	590.7	617.0	644.5				
18											
19		Net interest	11.1	0.0	0.0	0.0	0.0		FALSE	☐ Circular Toggle	
20		Profit before tax	99.5	516.0	540.1	565.3	591.7				

D19 fx =IF($I$19=1,D43,0)

Dynamic range names

What are dynamic range names?

A dynamic range is a range of cells that will automatically adjust to fit what is in the range. Dynamic ranges use the OFFSET function with an embedded COUNTA function to create the dynamic range formula. This formula is saved as a name for easy access, hence the term dynamic range name. You can use a dynamic range in any formula or function that uses ranges. However, because the range is dynamic, there is no need to update the range in the formula when the range changes.

Creating a dynamic range

The worksheet extract below contains a list of names and corresponding values.

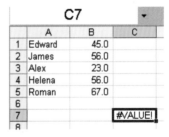

	A	B	C
1	Edward	45.0	
2	James	56.0	
3	Alex	23.0	
4	Helena	56.0	
5	Roman	67.0	
6			
7			#VALUE!
8			

C7

Cell C7 contains a dynamic range formula, which returns a #VALUE error because the range is not doing anything yet. Selecting a range of cells in Excel without putting the range into a function will always return a #VALUE error. The dynamic range formula has been written as:

```
=OFFSET(B1,0,0,COUNTA(B:B),1)
```

You will recall that the OFFSET function has the following syntax:

*=OFFSET(**reference**,**rows**,**columns**,[height],[width])*

In the example above, cell B1 is the reference cell. The row argument and column arguments are both 0. The optional height

 AdkinsMatchett&Toy

GRAND SCENARIOS

and width arguments are now being used. These arguments are used to make OFFSET return a range of cells rather than just a single cell. The height argument is a number that specifies how high the range should be and the width argument is a number that specifies how wide the range should be. The example above uses COUNTA(B:B) for the height argument in OFFSET to count how many cells have text or numbers in column B. This is what makes the range dynamic. The COUNTA function in the example above will return 5 because there are 5 cells with numbers in column B. The width argument is 1 because a range must be at least 1 column wide. As you add or remove data from column B, the COUNTA function will count the number of cells with data and the height of the range that OFFSET returns will update accordingly.

Like any range, a dynamic range is useless if used alone. It must be used in conjunction with a function or command in Excel. The example below shows a dynamic range being used in conjunction with the SUM function. The cell C7 contains the formula:

```
=SUM(OFFSET(B1,0,0,COUNTA(B:B),1))
```

	A	B	C	D
1	Edward	45.0		
2	James	56.0		
3	Alex	23.0		
4	Helena	56.0		
5	Roman	67.0		
6				
7			247.0	
8				

As you can see, the dynamic range is being used as the range argument of the SUM function. As you add values, the range of the SUM function will automatically adjust to include the new values because the range is dynamic. The values must be contiguous for the dynamic range to work.

	A	B	C
1	Edward	45.0	
2	James	56.0	
3	Alex	23.0	
4	Helena	56.0	
5	Roman	67.0	
6	Another	300.0	
7			547.0
8			

© Adkins, Matchett & Toy 2007   55   www.amttraining.com

Saving the dynamic range as a name

The easiest way to use your dynamic range in functions is to save the range as a name. To save the range as a name:

1. Choose Insert, Name, Define from the menu. The Define Name dialog box will appear.

2. Enter a name for the range in the Names in workbook box.

Names in workbook:

Dynamic

3. Input the dynamic range name formula in the Refers to box.

Refers to:

=OFFSET(Sheet2!$B$1,0,0,COUNTA(Sheet2!$B:$B),1)

Note: If you copy and paste the dynamic range name formula from the worksheet, make sure you absolute reference all the cell references as shown in the Refers to box above.

4. Choose OK to close the Define Name dialog box.

Now you can use the dynamic range name to access the name as shown with the SUM function below.

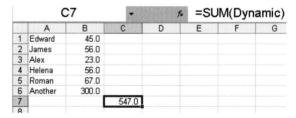

	A	B	C	D	E	F	G
1	Edward	45.0					
2	James	56.0					
3	Alex	23.0					
4	Helena	56.0					
5	Roman	67.0					
6	Another	300.0					
7			547.0				
8							

C7 — fx =SUM(Dynamic)

As you can see, cell C7 contains the SUM function with a dynamic range name called "Dynamic".

Modeling application

Dynamic range names are great when used in conjunction with the combo box on-sheet control. They make maintaining a list of inputs for the combo box very easy. Work through the following steps to see how this works.

1. Insert a new worksheet in the file to contain the combo box.

2. Enter your list of inputs for the combo box as shown below:

	A
1	London
2	New York
3	Paris
4	Hong Kong
5	

3. Choose Insert, Name, Define from the menu.

4. Type a name for the range in the Names in workbook box. For this example the name Dynamic was used.

Names in workbook:

Dynamic

5. Type the dynamic range name OFFSET formula in the Refers to box. In this example, the formula is:

`=OFFSET(Sheet2!$A$1,0,0,COUNTA(Sheet2!$A:$A),1)`

6. Choose OK to close the Define Name dialog box.

You have now created the dynamic range name. Now you can attach the name to a combo box. To do this, follow these steps:

1. Go to a separate worksheet in the same file.

2. Insert a combo box on the worksheet. To do this:

    a) Choose View, Toolbars, Forms from the menu to open the Forms toolbar. The Forms toolbar will appear.

    b) Select the combo box button on the Forms toolbar.

    c) Point somewhere in the worksheet (a crosshair symbol will appear) and click and drag to create a combo box.

3. Right click the new combo box and choose Format Control from the menu. The Format Control dialog box will appear.

4. Ensure the Control tab is active and input the dynamic range name in the Input range box. In this example, the dynamic range name is Dynamic.

Input range: Dynamic

5. Select other desired options and choose OK to close the Format Control dialog box.

When selecting the drop down box you will now see the inputs you defined in the other sheet. Furthermore, you can add or delete inputs in the other sheet and these will automatically be added to or deleted from the combo box.

DYNAMIC HEADINGS AND FOOTNOTES

When you change scenarios and methodologies in your model, the headings and footnotes that relate to the assumptions should also change. This can be done relatively easily using concatenation and the TEXT function.

CONCATENATION

Concatenation is a fancy term that describes the joining of two or more cells or text stings. Excel uses an ampersand as its concatenation operator. For example, if cell A1 contained the word "investment" and cell A2 contained the word "bank", the following formula would return "investmentbank".

```
=A1&A2
```

Notice that the two strings are joined together without a space. To add a space between the two words (i.e. "investment bank"), use the following formula:

```
=A1&" "&A2
```

You can also join text and values. For example, if cell A1 contains the string "The total is" and cell A2 contains the value 100, the following formula would return "The total is 100":

```
=A1&" "&A2
```

You can join text and formulas too. For example, if each cell in range A1:A5 contained the value 100, the following formula would return "The total is 500":

```
="The total is "&SUM(A1:A5)
```

So as you can see, to concatenate you simply separate each term with an ampersand (&).

There are three case functions that are very useful when creating dynamic headings. These are:

- LOWER
- UPPER
- PROPER

LOWER function

The LOWER function converts text to lower case. For example, if cell A1 contains the word "INVESTMENT", the following formula would return "investment".

```
=LOWER(A1)
```

UPPER function

The UPPER function converts text to upper case. For example, if cell A1 contains the word "investment", the following formula would return "INVESTMENT".

```
=UPPER(A1)
```

PROPER function

The PROPER function capitalizes the first letter in a text string and any other letters in text that follow any character other than a letter. It converts all other letters to lowercase letters. For example, if cell A1 contains the word "INVESTMENT BANK", the following formula would return "Investment Bank":

```
=PROPER(A1)
```

MODELING APPLICATION

Concatenation, case, and switch functions can be very powerful when used in the context of scenario management. For example, as you change scenarios in your model you will probably want your headings to change to reflect the new scenario.

In the worksheet below, the heading in cell A1 changes as the scenario choice changes in the model. At the moment, the best case scenario is selected.

	A	B	C	D	E	F	G
1	ABC COMPANY - *Base case*		Year 1	Year 2	Year 3	Year 4	Year 5
2							
3	Base case ▼						
4							
5	Base case		5.0%	5.0%	5.0%	5.0%	5.0%
6	Best case		10.0%	10.0%	10.0%	10.0%	10.0%
7	Worst case		1.0%	1.0%	1.0%	1.0%	1.0%
8							
9		1.0					
10							
11	Sales growth rate		5.0%	5.0%	5.0%	5.0%	5.0%
12							

Cell A1 contains the following formula:

```
="ABC COMPANY - "&CHOOSE(B9,B5,B6,B7)
```

The CHOOSE function returns the name of the case based on the scenario chosen using the drop down box. A more sophisticated formula would be:

```
="ABC COMPANY - "&UPPER(CHOOSE(B9,B5,B6,B7))
```

In this formula, the UPPER function has been wrapped around the CHOOSE function so that the CHOOSE function returns the name of the case in uppercase letters.

	B	C	D	E	F	G
1	ABC COMPANY - BASE CASE	Year 1	Year 2	Year 3	Year 4	Year 5
2						
3	Base case ▼					
4						
5	Base case	5.0%	5.0%	5.0%	5.0%	5.0%
6	Best case	10.0%	10.0%	10.0%	10.0%	10.0%
7	Worst case	1.0%	1.0%	1.0%	1.0%	1.0%
8						
9	1.0					
10						
11	Sales growth rate	5.0%	5.0%	5.0%	5.0%	5.0%

TEXT FUNCTION

The TEXT function is an essential ingredient when working with dynamic headings and footnotes. The TEXT function converts a value to a specific number format. The TEXT function has the following syntax:

=TEXT(value,format_text)

value   A numeric value; it can be a formula that evaluates to a numeric value or a reference to a cell containing a numeric value.

format_text   A number format input as a text string enclosed in quotation marks. You can see various number formats by selecting the Number, Date, Time, Currency, or Custom categories in the Category box of the Number tab in the Format Cells dialog box and viewing the formats displayed. You can also refer to chapter 1 for some information on number formats.

The following is an extract from a merger model. Cells B1, B4, and B5 contain the transaction closing date, the proportion of the purchase price financed by debt, and the proportion of the purchase price financed with equity respectively.

	A	B
1	Transaction date	12-Jul-07
2		
3	Financing:	
4	Debt	30.0%
5	Equity	70.0%
6		

The following formula would return the string "Purchase price has been financed with 0.3 equity":

```
="Purchase price has been financed with "&B4&"
debt"
```

As you can see cell B4 has been concatenated between two text strings. However, if you concatenate a number with text, the number will not be formatted. This is where the TEXT function comes in. You can use the TEXT function to format the concatenated number.

The following formula would return the string "Purchase price has been financed with 30% debt":

```
="Purchase price has been financed with
"&TEXT(B4,"0.0%")&" debt"
```

In the above example, the TEXT function would format the number relating to the proportion of debt financing as a percent.

Similarly with the transaction date, the following formula would return "Transaction closing date is 39275":

```
="Transaction closing date is "&B1
```

The formula returns the transaction date as a serial number. This is because a date in Excel is based on an underlying serial number.

When concatenating with dates, you must therefore use the TEXT function to format the date serial number as a date. The following formula would return "Transaction closing date is 12-Jul-07":

```
="Transaction closing date is "&TEXT(B1,"dd-mmm-
yy")
```

As you can see, the TEXT function formats the serial number as a date.

Sensitizing Your Work

INTRODUCTION

Sensitivity analysis is an essential part of many company valuation models. For example, in a discounted cash flow model you will use sensitivity analysis to see how different discount rates and growth rates affects the valuation. In a leveraged buyout model you will use sensitivity analysis to see how the purchase price of the business affects the returns to equity holders. Many other models will also use sensitivity analysis.

The easiest way to perform a sensitivity analysis in Excel is with data tables. This chapter is therefore devoted to building and working with data tables in Excel.

DATA TABLES

As mentioned above, data tables are handy tools for performing sensitivity analysis in a model. There are two types of data tables in Excel: one-input data tables and two-input data tables.

One-input data tables allow you to perform sensitivity analysis on one variable in a model. For example, one could see how the implied share price in a discounted cash flow model changes as the discount rate changes.

Two-input data tables allow you to perform sensitivity analysis on two variables in a model. For example, one could see how the implied share price in a discounted cash flow model changes as the discount rate and terminal growth rate change.

Data tables are very memory intensive due to the number of calculations Excel must perform to create them. If you use many data tables in your model, you will find the performance of your computer significantly inhibited. You should therefore not use data tables as if they are an infinite resource.

In order to illustrate the use of data tables, we are going to use the PMT function in Excel. The PMT function returns the payment for a loan based on constant payments and a constant interest rate. It has the following syntax:

=PMT(*rate,nper,pv,fv,type*)

rate   The interest rate for the loan.

nper   The total number of payments for the loan.

pv   The present value (the total amount that a series of future payments is worth now); also known as the principal.

fv   The future value (the cash balance you want to attain after the last payment is made). If fv is omitted, it is assumed to be zero, that is, the future value of the loan is 0.

type   The number 0 or 1; it indicates when payments are due: set type equal to 0 (or omit) if payments are due at the end of the period or 1 if payments are due at the beginning of the period.

Cell B4 in the worksheet extract below contains a PMT formula which returns the monthly payment necessary to amortize a $10,000 loan with an interest rate of 10% over a 3 year period. The PMT formula has been written as:

```
=PMT(B2/12,B3*12,-B1)
```

	A	B	C
1	Loan amount	10,000.0	
2	Interest rate	10.0%	
3	Term	3.0	
4	PMT	322.7	
5			

We will use this extract in order to discuss one-input and two-input data tables.

ONE-INPUT DATA TABLES

One-input data tables show the different results of a formula or function based on one input changing. For example, using the worksheet extract above, we may wish to see the monthly payments based on different loan amounts. One-input data tables can be vertical or horizontal.

Creating a vertical one-input data table

To create a vertical one-input data table, follow these steps:

1. Ensure you have set up a model with input cells feeding into a formula, similar to the extract above.

2. Enter the various input values that represent the changing desired input in a column. In the example below, these are various loan amounts in the range A7:A11.

	A	B
1	Loan amount	10,000.0
2	Interest rate	10.0%
3	Term	3.0
4	PMT	322.7
5		
6		
7	2,000.0	
8	4,000.0	
9	6,000.0	
10	8,000.0	
11	10,000.0	
12		

3. Link to the formula in the cell directly above and to the right of the input values. In our example, this is cell B6, which is linked to cell B4.

B6		▾		ƒx	=B4

	A	B	C	D	E
1	Loan amount	10,000.0			
2	Interest rate	10.0%			
3	Term	3.0			
4	PMT	322.7			
5					
6		322.7			
7	2,000.0				
8	4,000.0				
9	6,000.0				
10	8,000.0				
11	10,000.0				
12					

4. Select the rectangular area which contains the entries from the previous two steps. In this example, this is range A6:B11.

	A	B	C	D	
1	Loan amount	10,000.0			
2	Interest rate	10.0%			
3	Term	3.0			
4	PMT	322.7			
5					
6		322.7			
7	2,000.0				
8	4,000.0				
9	6,000.0				
10	8,000.0				
11	10,000.0				
12					
13					

5. Choose Data, Table from the menu. The Data Table dialog box will appear.

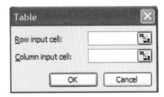

Because the inputs are in a column (in range A7:A11), you must specify the column input cell. Excel will substitute each input you supply into the column input cell you specify. The input cell you specify must feed either directly or indirectly into the formula linked to the data table. The data table will then return the corresponding results next to each input value.

6. Specify the column input cell. In this example, this is cell B1.

	A	B	C	D	E
1	Loan amount	10,000.0			
2	Interest rate	10.0%			
3	Term	3.0			
4	PMT	322.7			
5					
6					
7		322.7			
8	2,000.0				
9	4,000.0				
10	6,000.0				
11	8,000.0				
12	10,000.0				
13					
14					
15					

Table

Row input cell:

Column input cell: $B$1

OK   Cancel

7. Leave the Row input cell field empty.

8. Choose OK. The corresponding results will be returned.

	A	B
1	Loan amount	10,000.0
2	Interest rate	10.0%
3	Term	3.0
4	PMT	322.7
5		
6		322.7
7	2,000.0	64.5
8	4,000.0	129.1
9	6,000.0	193.6
10	8,000.0	258.1
11	10,000.0	322.7

Creating a horizontal one-input data table

The steps required to build a horizontal one-input data table are almost identical to those above:

1. Ensure you have set up a model with input cells feeding into a formula.

2. Enter the various input values that represent the changing desired input in a row. In the example below, these are various loan amounts in the range B7:F7.

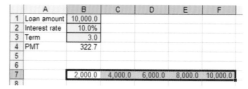

	A	B	C	D	E	F
1	Loan amount	10,000.0				
2	Interest rate	10.0%				
3	Term	3.0				
4	PMT	322.7				
5						
6						
7		2,000.0	4,000.0	6,000.0	8,000.0	10,000.0
8						

3. Link to the formula in the cell to the left and below the input values. In our example, this is cell A8, which is linked to cell B4.

A8			▼	*fx*	=B4	
	A	B	C	D	E	F
1	Loan amount	10,000.0				
2	Interest rate	10.0%				
3	Term	3.0				
4	PMT	322.7				
5						
6						
7		2,000.0	4,000.0	6,000.0	8,000.0	10,000.0
8	322.7					
9						

4. Select the rectangular area which contains the entries from the previous two steps. In this example, this is range A7:F8.

	A	B	C	D	E	F
1	Loan amount	10,000.0				
2	Interest rate	10.0%				
3	Term	3.0				
4	PMT	322.7				
5						
6						
7		2,000.0	4,000.0	6,000.0	8,000.0	10,000.0
8	322.7					
9						

5. Choose Data, Table from the menu. The Data Table dialog box will appear.

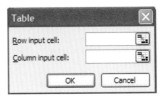

Because the inputs are in a row (in range B7:F7), you must specify a row input cell. Excel will substitute each input you supply into the row input cell you specify. The input cell you specify must feed either directly or indirectly into the formula linked to the data table. The data table will then return the corresponding results next to each input value.

6. Specify the row input cell. In this example, this is cell B1.

	A	B	C	D	E	F
1	Loan amount	10,000.0				
2	Interest rate	10.0%				
3	Term	3.0				
4	PMT	322.7				
5						
6						
7			2,000.0	4,000.0	6,000.0	8,000.0	10,000.0
8	322.7					

Table

Row input cell: $B$1

Column input cell:

OK   Cancel

7. Leave the Column input cell field empty.

8. Choose OK. The corresponding results are returned.

	A	B	C	D	E	F
1	Loan amount	10,000.0				
2	Interest rate	10.0%				
3	Term	3.0				
4	PMT	322.7				
5						
6						
7			2,000.0	4,000.0	6,000.0	8,000.0	10,000.0
8		322.7	64.5	129.1	193.6	258.1	322.7

TWO-INPUT DATA TABLES

Two-input data tables show the different results of a formula or function based on two inputs changing. For example, using the worksheet extract above, we may wish to see the monthly payments based on different loan amounts and different durations. To create a two-input data table, follow these steps:

1. Ensure you have set up a model with input cells feeding into a formula.

2. Enter the inputs that represent the first desired changing input in a column. In the extract below, these are different loan amounts entered into cells A7:A11.

	A	B	C
1	Loan amount	10,000.0	
2	Interest rate	10.0%	
3	Term	3.0	
4	PMT	322.7	
5			
6			
7	2,000.0		
8	4,000.0		
9	6,000.0		
10	8,000.0		
11	10,000.0		
12			

3. Enter the inputs that represent the second desired changing input in a row, which should be located immediately above and to the right of the column input cells. In the extract below, these inputs are the different loan terms entered in cells B6:F6.

	A	B	C	D	E	F	
1	Loan amount	10,000.0					
2	Interest rate	10.0%					
3	Term	3.0					
4	PMT	322.7					
5							
6		1.0	2.0	3.0	4.0	5.0	
7	2,000.0						
8	4,000.0						
9	6,000.0						
10	8,000.0						
11	10,000.0						
12							

4. Where the column input cells and row input cells intercept, create a link to the formula that will run the data table. In the worksheet extract below, the interception point is cell A6, which is linked to cell B4.

A6		▾		fx	=B4	

	A	B	C	D	E	F
1	Loan amount	10,000.0				
2	Interest rate	10.0%				
3	Term	3.0				
4	PMT	322.7				
5						
6	322.7	1.0	2.0	3.0	4.0	5.0
7	2,000.0					
8	4,000.0					
9	6,000.0					
10	8,000.0					
11	10,000.0					
12						

5. Select the rectangular area which contains the entries from the previous three steps. In this example, this is range A6:F11.

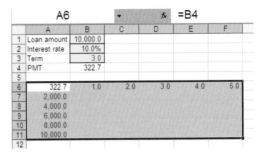

A6				▾	f_x =B4	
	A	B	C	D	E	F
1	Loan amount	10,000.0				
2	Interest rate	10.0%				
3	Term	3.0				
4	PMT	322.7				
5						
6	322.7	1.0	2.0	3.0	4.0	5.0
7	2,000.0					
8	4,000.0					
9	6,000.0					
10	8,000.0					
11	10,000.0					
12						

6. Choose Data, Table from the menu. The Data Table dialog box will appear.

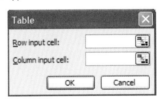

Because the inputs are in a row (in range B6:F6) and a column (in range A7:A11), you must specify a row input cell and a column input cell. Excel will substitute the row inputs you supply in the row input cell and the column inputs in the column input cell. As with one-input data tables, the row and column input cells you specify must feed either directly or indirectly into the formula linked to the data table. The data table will then return the corresponding results next to each input value.

7. Specify the row input cell. In this example, this is the term, which is in cell B3.

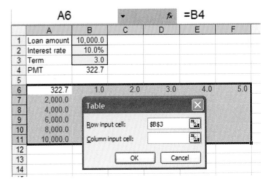

A6				▾	f_x =B4	
	A	B	C	D	E	F
1	Loan amount	10,000.0				
2	Interest rate	10.0%				
3	Term	3.0				
4	PMT	322.7				
5						
6	322.7	1.0	2.0	3.0	4.0	5.0
7	2,000.0					
8	4,000.0					
9	6,000.0					
10	8,000.0					
11	10,000.0					
12						
13						
14						

8. Specify the column input cell. In this example, this is the loan amount, which is in cell B1.

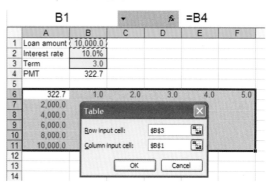

9. Choose OK. The corresponding results will be returned.

	A	B	C	D	E	F
1	Loan amount	10,000.0				
2	Interest rate	10.0%				
3	Term	3.0				
4	PMT	322.7				
5						
6	322.7	1.0	2.0	3.0	4.0	5.0
7	2,000.0	175.8	92.3	64.5	50.7	42.5
8	4,000.0	351.7	184.6	129.1	101.5	85.0
9	6,000.0	527.5	276.9	193.6	152.2	127.5
10	8,000.0	703.3	369.2	258.1	202.9	170.0
11	10,000.0	879.2	461.4	322.7	253.6	212.5

MODELING APPLICATION

As mentioned above, data tables are a common addition to financial models because they allow you to perform sensitivity analysis on a model's results. This section will look at using data tables with a discounted cash flow model.

The worksheet extract below is a discounted cash flow model for a fictitious business. In cell C30, the model calculates an enterprise value of $704m and assumes a terminal growth rate of 2% (cell C5) and a discount rate of10% (cell C4).

	A| B	C	D	E	F	G	H	
1	*Assumptions*							
2								
3	Tax rate	35.0%						
4	Discount rate	10.0%						
5	Terminal growth rate	2.0%						
6								
7	*Free Cash Flows*							
8								
9	Year count	0.0	1.0	2.0	3.0	4.0	5.0	
10	EBIT		90.0	91.8	93.6	95.5	97.4	
11	Tax		(31.5)	(32.1)	(32.8)	(33.4)	(34.1)	
12								
13	EBIAT		58.5	59.7	60.9	62.1	63.3	
14	Depreciation		12.8	13.1	13.3	13.6	13.9	
15	OWC		(1.5)	(1.5)	(1.6)	(1.6)	(1.6)	
16	Capital expenditure		(13.5)	(13.8)	(14.0)	(14.3)	(14.6)	
17	FCF		56.3	57.5	58.6	59.8	61.0	
18								
19	*Terminal value*							
20								
21	Perpetuity method						777.3	
22								
23	*Discounting model*							
24								
25	Discount factor		90.9%	82.6%	75.1%	68.3%	62.1%	
26	Present value of FCFs		51.2	47.5	44.0	40.8	37.9	
27								
28	SUM of PV of FCFs	221.4						
29	PV of terminal value	482.7						
30	Enterprise value	704.0						

This model could use a data table to see how changing the perpetuity growth rate and the discount rate will affect the enterprise valuation. The following steps must be taken to build this two-input data table:

1. Enter the various growth rates in a row. With this model, the growth rates will range from 1.5% to 2.5%, with 0.5% incremental steps in range C34:E34.

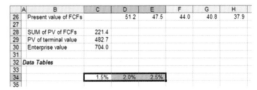

2. Enter the various discount rates in a column. With this model the discount rates will range from 9% to 11% with 0.5% incremental steps in range B35:B39.

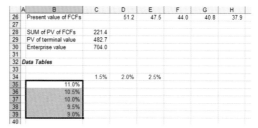

	A	B	C	D	E	F	G	H
26		Present value of FCFs		51.2	47.5	44.0	40.8	37.9
27								
28		SUM of PV of FCFs	221.4					
29		PV of terminal value	482.7					
30		Enterprise value	704.0					
31								
32		*Data Tables*						
33								
34				1.5%	2.0%	2.5%		
35		11.0%						
36		10.5%						
37		10.0%						
38		9.5%						
39		9.0%						
40								

3. Link to the enterprise value cell in cell B34.

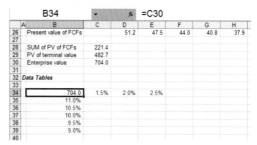

B34				f_x	=C30			
	A	B	C	D	E	F	G	H
26		Present value of FCFs		51.2	47.5	44.0	40.8	37.9
27								
28		SUM of PV of FCFs	221.4					
29		PV of terminal value	482.7					
30		Enterprise value	704.0					
31								
32		*Data Tables*						
33								
34		704.0	1.5%	2.0%	2.5%			
35		11.0%						
36		10.5%						
37		10.0%						
38		9.5%						
39		9.0%						
40								

4. Select the data table area, which is range B34:E39 in this example.

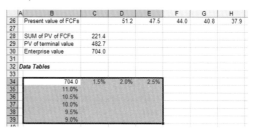

	A	B	C	D	E	F	G	H
26		Present value of FCFs		51.2	47.5	44.0	40.8	37.9
27								
28		SUM of PV of FCFs	221.4					
29		PV of terminal value	482.7					
30		Enterprise value	704.0					
31								
32		*Data Tables*						
33								
34		704.0	1.5%	2.0%	2.5%			
35		11.0%						
36		10.5%						
37		10.0%						
38		9.5%						
39		9.0%						

5. Choose <u>D</u>ata, <u>T</u>able from the menu.

6. Specify C5 as the row input cell and C4 as the column input cell.

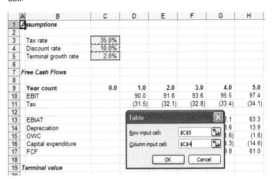

7. Choose OK to display the corresponding results.

	B	C	D	E	F
32	**Data Tables**				
33					
34	704.0	1.5%	2.0%	2.5%	
35	11.0%	602.3	625.8	652.1	
36	10.5%	635.9	662.6	692.7	
37	10.0%	673.4	704.0	738.7	
38	9.5%	715.6	751.0	791.4	
39	9.0%	763.5	804.6	852.1	
40					

Using the results of this data table, you may conclude that the discounted cash flow valuation range of this business is from $602.3m to $852.1m based on a discount rate range of 11% to 9% and a perpetuity growth rate range of 1.5% to 2.5%.

SENSITIZING DATA TABLE INPUT VALUES

It can be useful to link the row and column input values in your data table to the corresponding input values in the model. This is illustrated below using the discounted cash flow model from above.

The row input cells (range C38:E38) are the various perpetuity growth rates to sensitize. The column input cells (range B39:B43) are the various discount rates to sensitize.

	B	C	D	E	F	G
32	**Data Tables**					
33						
34	**Incremental changes:**					
35	Perpetuity growth rate	0.5%				
36	Discount rate	0.5%				
37						
38	704.0	1.5%	2.0%	2.5%		
39	11.0%					
40	10.5%					
41	10.0%					
42	9.5%					
43	9.0%					

Unlike the previous examples, the row and column input values are no longer hard inputs. Cell D38 is linked to cell C5 in the model, the perpetuity growth rate assumption.

D38 =C5

	A	B	C	D	E	F
31						
32		*Data Tables*				
33						
34		**Incremental changes:**				
35		Perpetuity growth rate	0.5%			
36		Discount rate	0.5%			
37						
38		704.0	1.5%	2.0%	2.5%	
39		11.0%				
40		10.5%				
41		10.0%				
42		9.5%				
43		9.0%				

The growth rates in cells E38 and C38 have been calculated using the growth rate in cell D38 and the perpetuity growth rate incremental change in cell C35.

E38 =D38+C35

	A	B	C	D	E	F
31						
32		*Data Tables*				
33						
34		**Incremental changes:**				
35		Perpetuity growth rate	0.5%			
36		Discount rate	0.5%			
37						
38		704.0	1.5%	2.0%	2.5%	
39		11.0%				
40		10.5%				
41		10.0%				
42		9.5%				
43		9.0%				

Cell B41 is linked to cell C4 in the model, the discount rate assumption in the model.

B41			▾		f_x	=C4

	A	B	C	D	E
31					
32		*Data Tables*			
33					
34		**Incremental changes:**			
35		Perpetuity growth rate	0.5%		
36		Discount rate	0.5%		
37					
38		704.0	1.5%	2.0%	2.5%
39		11.0%			
40		10.5%			
41		10.0%			
42		9.5%			
43		9.0%			

The discount rates in cells B39, B40, B42, and B43 have been calculated using the discount rate in cell B41 and the discount rate incremental change in cell B36.

B42			▾		f_x	=B41-$C$36	

	A	B	C	D	E	F
31						
32		*Data Tables*				
33						
34		**Incremental changes:**				
35		Perpetuity growth rate	0.5%			
36		Discount rate	0.5%			
37						
38		704.0	1.5%	2.0%	2.5%	
39		11.0%				
40		10.5%				
41		10.0%				
42		9.5%				
43		9.0%				

As usual, the formula to be sensitized is linked into the top left hand corner of this two-input data table. With this example, this formula is in cell B38 which is linked to the enterprise value cell C30.

If you run the Data, Table command with this example, the resulting sensitivity table will return incorrect results as you can see below.

This data table was created using C5 as the row input cell and C4 as the column input cell. This creates circularity in the table which Excel cannot resolve.

	A	B	C	D	E
32	*Data Tables*				
33					
34		**Incremental changes:**			
35		Perpetuity growth rate	0.5%		
36		Discount rate	0.5%		
37					
38		704.0	1.5%	2.0%	2.5%
39		11.0%	602.3	602.3	625.8
40		10.5%	572.1	572.1	592.9
41		10.0%	572.1	572.1	592.9
42		9.5%	602.3	602.3	625.8
43		9.0%	673.4	673.4	704.0

The circularity exists because the growth rate and discount rate input cells (C5 and C4 in this model) feed indirectly into the row input values (B39:B43) and column input values (C38:E38). When Excel creates the data table, it substitutes the row input values into the row input cell you specify, which is C5 in this example. Excel also substitutes the column input values into the column input cell you specify, which is C4. This is circular – the input cells are driving the input values and the input values are driving the input cells, as illustrated in the diagram below.

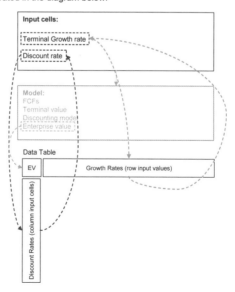

A solution to this problem is to use a master cell and clone cell data table structure to avoid the circularity issue described above. The input cells feed the clone cells. The clone cells feed the formula to sensitize and the master cells feed the row and column input values in the data table. This is illustrated with the diagram below.

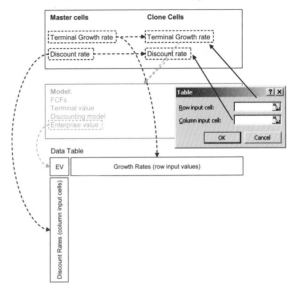

As you can see, the master cells directly feed the clone cells. The clone cells feed the various formulas in the model, which will feed the formula cell in the data table. The row and column input cells are the clone cells. The master cells no longer feed formulas in the model. They simply feed the row and column input values in the data table. With this structure, Excel will substitute the row and column input values into the clone cells. When this happens, the master cells, which feed the row and column input values in the data table are not affected because the master cells feed into the clone cells and not the other way around.

Let's apply this structure to our DCF model example. We'll do this through the following steps:

1. First, we'll create the clone cells. Do this by simply linking the clone cells to the master cells. In the worksheet below, D4 is linked to C4 and D5 is linked to C5.

	A	B	C	D	E
	D4		▾	*fx* **=C4**	
1		*Assumptions*			
2			Master	Clone	
3		Tax rate	35.0%		
4		Discount rate	10.0%	10.0%	
5		Terminal growth rate	2.0%	2.0%	
6					

2. Change all formulas in the main DCF model to refer to the clone cells.

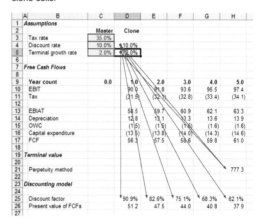

	B	C	D	E	F	G	H
1	*Assumptions*						
2		Master	Clone				
3	Tax rate	35.0%					
4	Discount rate	10.0%	10.0%				
5	Terminal growth rate	2.0%	2.0%				
6							
7	*Free Cash Flows*						
8							
9	Year count	0.0	1.0	2.0	3.0	4.0	5.0
10	EBIT		90.0	91.8	93.6	95.5	97.4
11	Tax		(31.5)	(32.1)	(32.8)	(33.4)	(34.1)
12							
13	EBIAT		58.5	59.7	60.9	62.1	63.3
14	Depreciation		12.8	13.1	13.3	13.6	13.9
15	OWC		(1.5)	(1.5)	(1.6)	(1.6)	(1.6)
16	Capital expenditure		(13.5)	(13.8)	(14.0)	(14.3)	(14.6)
17	FCF		56.3	57.5	58.6	59.8	61.0
18							
19	*Terminal value*						
20							
21	Perpetuity method						777.3
22							
23	*Discounting model*						
24							
25	Discount factor		90.9%	82.6%	75.1%	68.3%	62.1%
26	Present value of FCFs		51.2	47.5	44.0	40.8	37.9
27							

a) Change the growing perpetuity terminal value formula so that it refers to the discount rate and terminal growth rate in the clone cells as shown below:

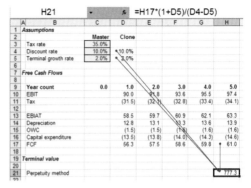

b) Change the discount factor in each projected year so that it now refers to the discount rate clone cell as shown below:

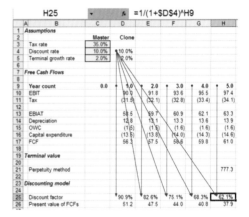

3. Ensure the row and column input values in the data table refer to the master cells. In the extract below, cell D38 is linked to C5 and cell B41 is linked to C4.

	A	B	C	D	E	F
1		*Assumptions*				
2			**Master**	Clone		
3		Tax rate	35.0%			
4		Discount rate	10.0%	10.0%		
5		Terminal growth rate	2.0%	2.0%		
6						
31						
32		*Data Tables*				
33						
34		**Incremental changes:**				
35		Perpetuity growth rate	0.5%			
36		Discount rate	0.5%			
37						
38		704.0	1.5%	2.0%	2.5%	
39		11.0%				
40		10.5%				
41		10.0%				
42		9.5%				
43		9.0%				
44						

Note: In this worksheet extract rows 7-30 are hidden.

4. Select the data table area.

	A	B	C	D	E	F
32		*Data Tables*				
33						
34		**Incremental changes:**				
35		Perpetuity growth rate	0.5%			
36		Discount rate	0.5%			
37						
38		704.0	1.5%	2.0%	2.5%	
39		11.0%				
40		10.5%				
41		10.0%				
42		9.5%				
43		9.0%				
44						

5. Choose Data, Table from the menu.

6. Specify the clone cells as the row and column input cells as shown below:

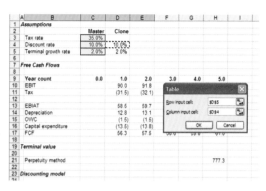

A	B	C	D	E	F	G	H	I
1	Assumptions							
2		Master	Clone					
3	Tax rate	35.0%						
4	Discount rate	10.0%	10.0%					
5	Terminal growth rate	2.0%	2.0%					
6								
7	Free Cash Flows							
8								
9	Year count	0.0	1.0	2.0	3.0	4.0	5.0	
10	EBIT		90.0	91.8				
11	Tax		(31.5)	(32.1)				
12								
13	EBIAT		58.5	59.7				
14	Depreciation		12.8	13.1				
15	OWC		(1.5)	(1.5)				
16	Capital expenditure		(13.5)	(13.8)				
17	FCF		56.3	57.5				
18								
19	Terminal value							
20								
21	Perpetuity method						777.3	
22								
23	Discounting model							

7. Choose OK. The data table should now populate with the correct values.

A	B	C	D	E
32	Data Tables			
33				
34	Incremental changes:			
35	Perpetuity growth rate	0.5%		
36	Discount rate	0.5%		
37				
38	704.0	1.5%	2.0%	2.5%
39	11.0%	602.3	625.8	652.1
40	10.5%	635.9	662.6	692.7
41	10.0%	673.4	704.0	738.7
42	9.5%	715.6	751.0	791.4
43	9.0%	763.5	804.6	852.1

You can cross check the values in the data table with the result in the main model to check that the results in the table are correct. With this example, the data table returns an enterprise value of $704m when the discount rate is 10% and the growth rate is 2%. Likewise, cell C30 in the main model returns the same enterprise value when a 2% growth rate and 10% discount rate are entered as the input assumptions as shown below.

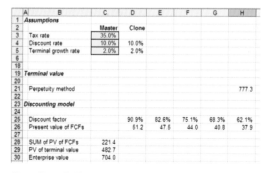

A	B	C	D	E	F	G	H
1	Assumptions						
2		Master	Clone				
3	Tax rate	35.0%					
4	Discount rate	10.0%	10.0%				
5	Terminal growth rate	2.0%	2.0%				
6							
18							
19	Terminal value						
20							
21	Perpetuity method						777.3
22							
23	Discounting model						
24							
25	Discount factor		90.9%	82.6%	75.1%	68.3%	62.1%
26	Present value of FCFs		51.2	47.5	44.0	40.8	37.9
27							
28	SUM of PV of FCFs	221.4					
29	PV of terminal value	482.7					
30	Enterprise value	704.0					

Note: Rows 7-17 in this worksheet extract are hidden.

Protecting Your Work

INTRODUCTION

Excel offers a number of ways to protect your work. The levels of protection range from preventing someone from seeing a formula you have written to preventing someone from accessing your file.

In this chapter, we will explore the different types of protection that Excel provides. We will focus on the following 5 areas:

- Hiding formulas
- Protecting cells and ranges
- Protecting the workbook structure
- Preventing changes from being saved
- Preventing access to a workbook

HIDING FORMULAS

Sometimes your models will contain proprietary formulas that you don't want other users to see. When you hide a formula, the formula bar will appear blank even when you have clicked on a cell that contains a formula. To hide formulas in your model, follow these steps:

1. Select the cells containing formulas you want to hide.

2. Choose Format, Cells from the menu. The Format Cells dialog box will appear.

3. Choose the Protection tab.

4. Check the Hidden check box.

5. Choose OK to close the Format Cells dialog box.

6. Choose Tools, Protection, Protect Sheet from the menu. The Protect Sheet dialog box will appear.

7. Specify a password if desired. If you specify a password, you will have to confirm the password entered.

8. Choose OK.

When you protect the sheet, you'll notice that you will not be able to amend any of the cells as they are locked by default. The next section addresses how to lock and unlock cells in a workbook.

To unhide the formulas, choose Tools, Protection, Unprotect Sheet from the menu. You may need to supply a password if a password was specified when protecting the sheet.

PROTECTING CELLS AND RANGES

In order to protect the formula structure of your model, you may wish to only allow users to change input cells and not formula cells. To do this:

1. Ensure the sheet is unprotected.

2. Select the input cells you DON'T want to protect.

3. Choose Format, Cells from the menu. The Format Cells dialog box will appear.

4. Choose the Protection tab.

5. Uncheck the Locked check box.

6. Choose OK to close the Format Cells dialog box.

7. Choose Tools, Protection, Protect Sheet from the menu. The Protect Sheet dialog box will appear.

8. Specify a password if desired. If you specify a password, you will have to confirm the password entered.

9. Choose OK.

Now you will only be able to change the cells you formatted as unlocked. Once again, to unlock the sheet so that users can amend all formulas, choose Tools, Unprotect Sheet from the menu.

Sometimes you may want to allow certain users to change the contents of some cells in your model. You can do this by supplying them with a password. When they want to change the cells in question, they must enter the password. To do this, follow these steps:

1. Ensure the cells that you would like to allow certain people access to are locked. To do this:

    a) Select the cells.

    b) Choose Format, Cells from the menu.

    c) Choose the Protection tab.

    d) Ensure the Locked check box is checked.

2. Select the cells that you would like to allow certain people access to.

3. Choose Tools, Protection, Allow Users to Edit Ranges from the menu. The Allow Users to Edit Ranges dialog box will appear.

4. Choose New. The New Range dialog box will appear.

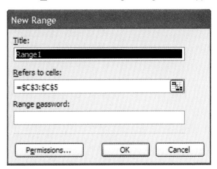

5. Type a name for the range in the Title text box.

6. Type a password in the Range password box.

7. Choose OK. The Confirm Password dialog box will appear.

8. Retype the password in the Confirm Password dialog box.

9. Choose OK. The Allow Users to Edit Ranges dialog box will appear.

10. Choose the Protect Sheet button. The Protect Sheet dialog box will appear.

11. Specify a password if desired.

12. Choose OK to close the Protect Sheet dialog box.

When attempting to change the cells in the range specified, the user will now be prompted to type a password. If the correct password is entered, the user will be able to change the cells in question. If an incorrect password is entered, the user will not be able to change the cells. To deactivate this functionality, simply unprotect the sheet using Tools, Protection, Unprotect Sheet in the menu.

PROTECTING THE WORKBOOK STRUCTURE

When you protect the workbook structure, users can't add or delete sheets. To protect the workbook structure, follow these steps:

1. Choose Tools, Protection, Protect Workbook from the menu. The Protect Workbook dialog box will appear.

2. Ensure the Structure check box is checked.

3. Enter a password is desired.

4. Choose OK.

To deactivate this feature, choose Tools, Protection, Unprotect Workbook from the menu and enter a password if necessary.

PREVENTING CHANGES FROM BEING SAVED

Sometimes you will want to prevent users from saving changes to the model. To do this:

1. Ensure the file you want to protect is open and active.

2. Choose Tools, Options from the menu.

3. Select the Security tab.

4. Enter a password in the Password to modify text box.

File sharing settings for this workbook
Password to modify: [   ]

5. Choose OK.

6. Confirm the password.

7. Choose OK.

8. Save and close the file.

The next time the file is opened, the user will be presented with the following dialog box:

If the correct password is entered in the Password text box, the user will be able to make changes to the file. Alternatively, when opening the file, the user can choose the Read Only button. This would open the file in Read Only mode. In this mode, the user would have to save any changes under a different file name.

To deactivate this functionality, open the file in full access mode and delete the password from the Security tab of Tools, Options.

PREVENTING ACCESS TO A WORKBOOK

Sometimes you will only want certain people to access a model. This can be achieved by password protecting the workbook in question and giving the password to authorized users only. To password protect the model:

1. Ensure the workbook file is open and active.

2. Choose Tools, Options from the menu.

3. Select the Security tab.

4. Enter a password in the Password to open text box.

Password to open: [   ]

5. Choose OK.

6. Confirm the password.

7. Choose OK.

8. Close the file.

When the file is opened again, the user will be prompted to enter a password. The correct password must be entered to access the file. To deactivate this functionality, open the file and delete the password from the Security tab of Tools, Options.